Driving Your Way to Success

The 7 Day Plan to Reaching Your Forex Trading Goals

Published by:

Currex Investment Services Inc. (d.b.a. Forexmentor.com)

Revision Date: April, 2011

Legal Notices & Disclaimer

Trading currencies on margin involves a high level of risk which may not be suitable for all investors. Leverage can work against you just as easily as it can work for you. Before deciding to trade currencies you should carefully consider your trading and financial objectives, level of experience and appetite for risk. The possibility exists that you could sustain a loss of some, or possibly all of your trading capital. Therefore, you should not fund a trading account with money that you cannot afford to lose. It is recommended that you seek advice from an accredited financial advisor if you have any doubts as to whether currency trading is right for you. No guarantee or representation is offered or implied as to the trading results that may be attained by applying concepts presented herein. Any losses incurred by traders unsuccessful in applying these ideas or methods are the sole responsibility of the trader and David J. Deming and Currex Investment Services, Inc. (d.b.a. Forexmentor) and their principals, contractors and assigns will be held safe and indemnified from prosecution in any form.

Foreword

By Vic Noble – FX Coach at Forexmentor.com

The trading world has been flooded with so many systems, approaches, and methodologies over the years, yet so very few people are actually able to use the plethora of information to consistently profit from the Forex markets. Do you ever wonder why that is?

At this very moment, whether you know it or not, you hold something very special in your hands. This book is about the most important factor in trading—you.

I have had the pleasure of working with Dave Deming for many years now, and he has stood out as a unique person. I say that because he is one of the few to truly realize that the most important "system" that any of us can learn about is ourselves.

Dave has become a student of himself. He has learned what makes him tick, why he has success, failure, and what they mean.

I have been coaching traders for many years. In my experience, most aspiring traderse can be taught to understand the technicals and fundamentals. But what they fail to realize is that this information alone is not enough to become successful. Dave has fully understood and embraced that truth.

You have the power to decide on whatever it is that you want in your life. And if being a consistently profitable trader is part of your plan, I encourage in the strongest possible way to make a decision right now—make up your mind that you are going to harness the psychological tools and invaluable trading tips that Dave Deming has used to propel his trading to the next level.

I truly hope you find this book as inspirational as I have. It taps into the true Holy Grail of trading—understanding yourself.

Vic Noble
FX Coach – Forexmentor.com

Introduction

Whether you enjoy trading stocks, commodities, futures, S&P E-minis, U.S. Treasuries, spot foreign currencies or options, it is my sincere desire that this book will dramatically improve the mental aspect of your trading which will lead to significant improvement in your trading results.

There are no shortcuts to success in trading, but there are also no shortcuts to success in sports, medicine, law, engineering, parenting, being a spouse or serving as the coach of a youth sports team. Even though there are no shortcuts, there is a proven path to reaching the success you are searching for in your trading. Success is a byproduct of hard work, the willingness to learn from those who have already succeeded, being disciplined every day in your thoughts and actions and continuing to learn and refine the skills necessary to excel. This book details the path which I have taken for the last 3 ½ years. It is my desire to offer specific recommendations so that you can lay out a solid, specific and detailed game plan to reach your trading goals. Along the way, you will also see how the principles in this book apply not only in trading, but also to every area of your life where you're striving to improve your current results and move closer to excellence.

A key element of the 7 Day Plan I'll describe later in this book is the fine system for any violations of my weekly plan. Fines each week are contributed to various charitable organizations. In the interest of continuing to help a very worthwhile charity, St. Jude Children's Hospital in Memphis, Tennessee is the designated charity for this book. St. Jude is recognized internationally as a pioneer in research and the treatment of children with cancer and other catastrophic diseases. Since they opened their doors in 1962, St. Jude has treated children from all 50 states in the United States and from around the world. St. Jude is the only pediatric cancer research center where families are not asked to pay for any treatment not covered by insurance.

As you'll see in this book or as you'll learn from talking with me about my family, golf is a very important part of our lives. My oldest of five sons plays golf in college; our high school junior is beginning his search for a college golf team. Every year the PGA Tour hosts a tournament in Memphis to benefit St. Jude. This year's FedEx St. Jude Classic is scheduled for June 9-12, 2011. This tournament has raised over $24 million for St. Jude since 1970. My wife and I are very blessed to have five healthy children. With the strong link between the great game of golf and St. Jude, it will be my honor to contribute 10% of the sales proceeds of this book to this fabulous hospital. For more information, and to see how you can be a part of the miracles that St. Jude makes happen every year, please visit www.stjude.org.

Dave Deming

"Improving trading through promoting traders' personal and psychological development."

Acknowledgements

A special word of thanks to my wife - Brandy and to my sons - Taylor, Peyton, Kendal, Jackson and Sadler for their support and patience while I studied the Forex markets and then spent time to write this book. "The book", as we call it, has been greatly anticipated for many months now.

Thanks also to Vic Jung and Vic Noble for their time in reviewing and editing this book and for their ideas and suggestions on turning this idea into what you now hold in your hands. Thanks as well to Shirley Hudson for her review of an early draft and for her comments which clearly improved the content of the book. Shirley's work ethic is extremely motivating and her dedication to organizing the Coach's Corner archives makes them one of the most valuable tools which Forexmentor offers their members.

A final word of thanks to the many friends I've met from around the world through Coach's Corner and LiveConnect. Your energy and passion for learning and trading inspires me every day.

Table of Contents

I. Achieving Competency

The Journey Begins — Taking the first steps toward the universal concept of mastery

"I wake up; I make some money, and then go play for the rest of the day." I came across this statement in a trading magazine article that I read in spring, 2007. It was an article about the daily life of a well-known currency trader. It was very intriguing and appealing to me to say the least. What a lifestyle! Maybe currency trading was the way to reach my financial goals. I didn't know it at the time but I had just begun a long journey. This was the start of my struggle to understand and master the psychological skills required to become a successful trader. It was the beginning of my journey to learn why and how I thought the way that I did in past trading experiences and what changes I must make in order to succeed in trading. Whether one trades currencies, stocks, bonds, options, or any other financial instrument, there are some very certain principles or laws which must be learned and mastered to increase one's odds of survival. I was about to learn though that the most important laws concern the psychological side of trading and not the technical side of trading.

In the past, my stock trading results had been, for the most part, very modest. However, the reality of closing out a trade and then having to wait for the settlement date to pass three business days later was not only annoying, but prevented me from taking on additional trades. Many days, it was also difficult for me to follow stocks because of my job and family commitments. Nevertheless, I was very intrigued by the idea of trading with cash in a 24 hour market environment driven by economics and political forces on an international scale. With undergraduate degrees in political science and economics, followed by a law degree, dealing with the dynamics of market fundamentals of currency trading was a perfect fit for my background.

After investigating the currency markets and how currencies are traded, I began my search for a trading platform. I reviewed several platforms, but found some to be very balky and illogical – too many steps required to take action. Because my days are fast-paced, I wanted the ability to move quickly. Unfortunately, I incorrectly perceived currency trading as a split-second trading environment where speed of entries and exits were critical to my success. In retrospect, this completely incorrect belief and assumption would very quickly expose my underlying impulsive tendencies in my trading decision-making process. I would eventually learn that I must take into account my behavioral tendencies and how they will undoubtedly influence my trading.

My initial training in Forex (FX) trading was by way of a cursory training course and a 30-day "demo account" – the real trading platform with not so real money – and lots of it! Generally, most Forex dealers will provide you with an account balance of $50,000.00 or more of "play money" to practice trading. Demo accounts are an excellent place to test a new trade set-up a trader is considering using or, alternatively, to build confidence in a set-up a trader has decided to follow. However, demo accounts can, unfortunately, create a false sense of confidence in one's trading skills. Without real money on the line, human emotions such as fear and greed rarely have an opportunity to surface. With only play money at risk, a loss may not have any educational value. There may also be a tendency to engage in sloppy, undisciplined trading or over-trading in the pursuit of a quick "profit" in the account. It's far too easy with a demo account not to worry about risk management and trade management. It actually can instill bad trading habits. Finally, self-sabotage issues resulting from any underlying subconscious issues involving money may not come into play with demo trading.

In any event, armed with a demo account and a 30-day introductory FX training course, my currency education was underway. At the time, the concepts I was being taught seemed very difficult, but that was many thousands of hours ago. As with any new sport, hobby, or even a profession, competency in currency trading would take some time to begin to attain.

Malcolm Gladwell uncovers the mystery of the mastery benchmark in his New York Times bestseller Outliers (New York: Little, Brown and Co. 2008). Although talent and having special opportunities are important steps to success, Gladwell makes it very clear that the most important key to success from mastery is old-fashioned hard work. He cites psychologist K. Anders Ericsson's study at the Academy of Music in Berlin which found that future music teachers had only practiced 4000 hours on their instrument by the age of twenty, while very good students had logged 8000 hours of practice. The best musicians at the Academy, "the students with the potential to become world-class soloists", had notched 10,000 hours of practice time already by the time they were twenty. Outliers, pp. 38-39. Gladwell goes on to study The Beatles, chess expert Bobby Fisher, Steve Jobs and Paul Allen (Apple), Bill Gates (Microsoft) and Bill Joy (co-founder of Sun Microsystems; rewrote Java software) as examples of elite performers who all paid their dues and logged 10,000 quality hours and finely honed their skills to become masters at their crafts.

Gladwell quotes neurologist Daniel Levitin:

The emerging picture from such studies is that ten thousand hours is required to achieve the level of mastery associated with being a world-class expert –in anything. Outliers, p. 40.

At the time I began trading currencies, I literally knew no one in the world who was also trading currencies. I knew no one who had already put in even 10 hours, much less their 10,000 hours to become a "world-class expert" as discussed in Outliers. (Outliers is not a book about trading, but it is a book about the principles of success and what it takes to excel in any field). I knew no one to discuss currency trading with, to learn from, to ask questions, or to just listen to at times when listening was what I really needed. In my situation, I was flying solo and blazing (at least trying to) my own trail in the Forex wilderness. I could read everything I wanted on the internet, stare at charts all day and all night and make correct and incorrect decisions based on my miniscule level of expertise, but there was no one available to train, assist, and develop me as a trader – in other words, I had no one to mentor me in the learning process.

II. Forex Trading Before Forexmentor.com

Demo to Live in 30 Days — Transitioning to live training; not always a smooth road

After successfully completing the four-week series of lessons in the introductory training course my broker offered, I was completely ready (so I thought) for successful currency trading. A series of e-mails from the broker with whom I traded on the demo account persuasively laid out just how easy it would be to move to real trading. This time, though, it was with real money. The thought of launching my new Forex (Fx) trading career was truly energizing. I couldn't wait to get started on building my fortune. In retrospect, there were several major problems, though, that would impede my trading at the outset.

First, I did not have a specific trade set-up that I was going to use on a consistent basis in my trading. The introductory course had taught only the very basics of price movement, but had not taught me a dependable, reliable set-up that I could use to narrow my focus in my trading. Without a consistent set-up to watch for and with having confidence in that set-up, my early trading was not successful.

Second, my level of FX competency was so very low that I didn't even know how much I didn't know – there was so much more to learn on the road to 10,000-hour mastery. Most importantly, I had no one to talk with, to ask questions or learn from to increase my level of competency and my trading skills. The school of hard knocks and OJT (on-the-job training) were my teachers for far too long.

Third, one of the biggest holes in my trading skill set was the unawareness of the great importance of support and resistance on higher timeframes such as daily, weekly, and monthly charts. These are the timeframes that determine the market's trend. The 5 minute, 15 minute, and 1 hour timeframes can contain the "noise" or whippiness that isn't seen on larger timeframe charts. The attached charts (*Figures 1-4* at the end of the book) show the difference between lower timeframes and higher timeframes.

Trading intraday on the lower timeframe charts would subject my trades to price spikes that can occur as often as the wind blows on some days. I would learn later in my trading education that relying on higher timeframe charts would let me take advantage of the very important support and resistance principles as well as trading with the prevailing trend of the market.

Finally, and most importantly, as I'll layout in this book, I did not possess the correct mental or psychological skills which successful traders use in their trading. So, how was I able to trade without a specific system and no awareness of the importance of determining the prevailing trend, much less following it in a day trading environment?

Well, not real well as I discovered! My trading performance can best be described as inconsistent and mediocre. My approach in finding set-ups was very unreliable. I based almost all of my trading decisions on five minute charts. Entries based on these charts were not based on the highest probabilities possible. My trades based on five minute charts might only last a few minutes as price often jumped around after my entry to hit my stop and take me out of the trade. I didn't know the term at the time, but I "blew out" my extremely small starting account based on my trading of the five minute charts.

I learned about the importance of economic news announcements in my introductory currency trading class. On the web, there are many places to find daily economic news items for any given day. However, the best website that I've come across so far is www.forexfactory.com. This website is not only user friendly, dependable and accurate, it contains direct links to news items that develop throughout the trading day.

By reviewing its system of tiered announcements (based on the expected impact on the markets), a day trader can avoid being blown out of a trade by knowing ahead of time about the possible knee-jerk reaction to the latest news announcements. On the other hand, these news announcements may, in fact, lead a trader to enter a trade based on better than expected (BTE) or worse than expected (WTE) economic announcements. There are other more dangerous ways to use this information. Trading after a news announcement and after the market digests and reacts to the news is one thing. Trading in front of the news announcement is an entirely different matter.

At the time that I began currency trading, the world investment environment was one of taking on risk, i.e., low risk aversion. The United States and worldwide stock markets were climbing ever higher. The currencies that carried high levels of interest rates were also advancing at a very steady pace. Purchasing a high interest currency by selling a lower interest currency could result in profits from both the appreciation of the higher interest currency along with daily interest payments on the "spread" or difference between the interest rates of the two currencies. For example, currencies such as the Australian Dollar ("the Aussie") and the New Zealand Dollar ("the Kiwi") were appreciating very rapidly against the Japanese Yen, the U.S. Dollar and other "safe" or lower interest rate currencies because these currencies carried interest rates that were much higher than the currencies they were paired against.

For example, when I started currency trading, the central banks of Australia and New Zealand, in an effort to slow inflation, were systematically raising interest rates on their currencies. As illustrated by this chart, these two high interest currencies were becoming increasingly sought out as investment vehicles because of their interest rate increases:

RBA		RBNZ	
8/8/07	6.5%	6/7/07	8.0%
11/7/07	6.75%	7/26/07	8.25%
2/6/08	7.0%		
3/5/08	7.25%		

(www.rba.gov.au)   (www.rbnz.govt.nz)

I began currency trading in May, 2007. As you can see from this chart, in the low risk aversion market at that time, it was a sure bet that when there was a central bank meeting in these countries and an interest rate announcement, rates would move higher.

The immediate reaction to such an announcement would be a quick spike up in the price of the Aussie and the Kiwi against the U.S. Dollar or the Japanese Yen in particular. This led to a very predictable profit if I bought the Aussie or Kiwi a few minutes before the interest rate announcement. Armed with the exact time of the announcement from forexfactory.com, and the consensus of "experts" and economists around the world, this was one of my favorite early trading strategies. If I set a reasonable profit target, the interest rate spike-up would always lead to a quick profit in minutes, if not, seconds. "I get up, I make some money, and go play" was just as easy as it sounded! But what if the experts were wrong? Not to be – at least not yet.

Other news announcements such as retail sales, unemployment numbers, etc. led to far less predictable economic news trading results. The lure of quick profits, especially in a market open in the evening, after my work day was over, made Aussie and Kiwi trades very appealing.

As I explored this new world of Forex trading, I learned very quickly that certain pairs moved rapidly and other pairs crawled along. A currency paired with the Japanese Yen could move very quickly although some of these pairs tend to move faster than others. By nature, I can be impatient at times so speed of movement was much more appealing to me. One morning, very early in the day, I developed a method (I thought) for trading one of these pairs. Using my prior training in candles while trading stocks and what the currency training class taught me about oscillators and moving averages, I came up with "a system." In a matter of only 30 minutes, I closed out a trade with a 100 pip profit. 100 pips is a very good week in Forex trading and I had pulled it off with my new system in only 30 minutes. This pair performed exactly as I predicted by my system and it raced to my profit target. How could it get better? Why not (be greedy and) go for a repeat? And repeat it did – 100 pips of movement again. Too bad it went against me this time. This pair was very volatile, and it reached my 100 pip stop almost as quickly as it had reached my 100 pip profit target. This was my introduction to the Pound/Yen (GBP/JPY) currency pair. This nasty pair should never be traded by a beginning currency trader. In fact, I know a professional trader who doesn't trade this pair at all. Another lesson learned the hard way. Greed and wanting to be right twice lead to a break even day.

As I mentioned, Asian session trading had its appeals because the Asian market at opens the same time as the end of my work day in the U.S. One night, I discovered another "system" on 5-minute charts with the AUD/GBP pair, GBP/JPY's cousin as far as volatility goes. I traded multiple times that night and after all the dust settled on my many trades, it was a break even night at best. The rapid movement of this pair, especially on five minute charts, was too much for my system to handle.

Despite the fact that my trading losses were not always the result of knowledge or technical information issues, I now made an enormous wrong turn in the road at this point. Determined to minimize losses and maximize profits, I concluded that I needed to know more about the markets in order to become a successful currency trader. To learn more, I immersed myself in even more technical and chart training. In the advanced courses (i.e., expensive) that I took next, I learned about 5-minute moving average crossover systems, 5-minute slow stochastics entries, how to trade off the news, stochastic/ADX trading and many other complicated and detailed trading systems. Another course emphasized how important it was for a trader to use as many oscillators and technical indicators as possible and to load their charts full of these lines, bars, etc. to know when to enter and exit a trade. Looking back now at the thick notebooks I have from these classes, it's really amazing that I could even enter a trade after these courses because there were so many steps required to take a trade.

As Mark Douglas stresses in Trading in The Zone (New York: Prentice Hall Press 2000), traders don't make more money as a result of more detailed analysis. Learning more about the markets does not, according to Mark, necessarily make it easier and more profitable to trade. In fact, the more a trader seeks absolute knowledge about the markets, they will actually impede trading and negatively affect their trading results. In my case, this was no doubt true.

As my day timer sheets and my trade sheets at the time show in *Figures 5-7* (end of the book), I was on a mission to thoroughly keep track of and "know" the markets plus the many pairs I was following. I was watching a myriad of currency pairs and tracking prices throughout the day and night; watching the VIX; watching the equity markets around the world; and watching U.S. equity futures from Asia, overnight through Europe and into the New York opening. I was also watching the price of oil, gold and other commodities. *Figure 6*, my 8/12/07 trade sheet for the GBP/CHF shows that I was following these factors for trending pairs: Rising/falling support and resistance lines, ADX; watching for RSI, MACD or stochastic divergence; fibonacci lines, keeping an eye on five moving averages; risk reversals and the 7 Day rule (average true range). If that wasn't enough already, for a range-bound pair, I was watching: ADX, RSI and Stochastics for any signs of divergence; Bollinger bands, support and resistance; MACD and the risk reversals table. Over three years after the fact, I absolutely can't tell you how in the world I used all of this information to decide when to trade. But, I must have felt that I knew the markets!

How could I not know everything there was to know when my charts were full of this information? As further notes on the trade sheet reveal, to make absolutely sure that I knew everything, I was also watching candle action and the parabolic SAR.

The 10/1/07 day timer sheet shows that I was trying to track the daily trend of the 10 currencies that I was following at that time. *Figure 7* shows how I was tracking prices for many currencies. By noting price at various times in the 24 hr trading day, I was trying to see what pairs were stronger on a given day. At the time, I didn't know what to call these insane efforts, but I was starting to learn about inter-market analysis and the risk investment environment for the day. I've recently learned a much faster way to determine the status of the risk investment environment from Ashraf Laidi. He referred me to a very useful website called: www.finviz.com (click on the Futures tab) which provides an excellent graphical illustration of investors' sentiments on commodities, currencies and equities on any given day. This is a ten second, visual method to determine the day's risk environment at a glance. While this type of market information is useful, the market overload and technical/oscillator immersion that I was engaging in went way beyond the degree of market knowledge required to be successful in currency trading. What I needed at this point in my trading was training on how to consistently approach trading every day.

III. Learning How to Trade to Succeed

How leaving the country quickly corrected my approach to trading

Now the road was about to take another turn and point me directly to where I will remain for the rest of my Forex trading career. Some background is important though to understand how life (the road) had brought me to where I was at this point in my trading. Several years before I started trading currencies, a good friend recommended one of the first books that I read on stock trading--Toni Turner's A Beginner's Guide to Short-Term Trading (Avon: Adams Media, 2002). Steve Nison wrote the forward to that book. There is a small section in Toni's book which briefly discussed "candles", so this book provided my introduction to this concept. Steve Nison is viewed worldwide as the expert in candlestick charting and the psychology involved with candle patterns. Steve introduced the Western world to this Japanese charting system after he studied candles for many years. He is the authority in the world on candles. Contrary to standard bar charts, with candles, traders can obtain a crucial insight into where price may be going. More importantly, candles show what the market thinks about price movement that has already occurred. For example, even if price made a new high or a new low, where price actually closed and the force of the movement of price from the new high/new low to the closing price tells a lot about the strength of that move for the period of the candle, e.g., 15 minute, 1 hour, 4 hour, daily, et cetera. With this understanding of the significance of candles versus bar charts, I began to study candles in further detail. Over time, I added several Steve Nison books and courses to my trading library. (Recommended courses are listed in the Bibliography). I also subscribed to Steve's free video newsletter which highlights current market developments or an issue involving the psychology of candles. (Sign up on www.candlecharts.com). (In early February, 2011, Steve introduced a new website devoted exclusively to currency trading: www.nisonfx.com. Make sure to review the video on Advantages of Nison Candlesticks for FX Traders). Through studying candles, I learned that they are especially suited to send signals about the market's psychology. The shape of certain candles or candle patterns may signal acceptance of a price move, rejection of that move or the possibility of an impending reversal of price.

Because of my association with candlecharts.com, in spring, 2008, I received an e-mail from Candlecharts describing a seminar scheduled on April 5, 2008, in Toronto, Canada. The session featured two speakers – Steve Nison and Peter Bain. According to the e-mail, Peter was involved with a company which focused on educating Forex traders. Fortunately for me, without hesitating, I immediately signed up for the seminar. It was on the weekend, which made travel very easy for me. Admittedly, my initial interest in attending the seminar was to learn more about candles. I was still in the mode of trying to over learn the markets so that I could be "right" more often. I was convinced that more candle knowledge was what I needed to improve my trading results.

I flew to Toronto late Friday after work. The seminar was only on Saturday and I picked a return flight home late Saturday night so I could spend Sunday with my family. I really wanted the seminar schedule to have candles in the morning and the FX talk in the afternoon. Because of my flight schedule, I was going to have to leave the seminar one hour early. After all, it was the candle knowledge that I needed to improve my trading. Fortunately, the schedule was the exact opposite of where I felt the road should take me.

After a quick breakfast in the hotel, I found the seminar meeting room.

Before the seminar even began, I received the first of many lessons I was to learn in the months and years ahead regarding just how much Forexmentor was to change the direction of my trading. I've heard in many personal development programs in the past that winners stick out their hand first and introduce themselves to strangers. I saw this in action that morning in Toronto. Before we began, Peter Bain, the Forex speaker, started briskly walking up and down the aisles of seats to introduce himself to the seminar guests. I've never seen that at any meeting I've ever been a part of in the past. He looked each person squarely in the eye and sincerely, and very genuinely, told each one of us that he wanted to do whatever he could to help us succeed in our trading. That act of humility and sincerity has been repeated over and over again in my association with everyone at Forexmentor. The dominant attitude of everyone I've dealt with is one of professionalism, patience, and a strong desire to teach, coach, and train aspiring currency traders.

Peter ran hard in his morning presentation as he had a lot to teach us in half a day. For the first time, I learned about the concept of pivot points, buying and selling zones and I also learned the critical importance of support and resistance on higher timeframes. There was one suggestion, though, that Peter made that impacts my trading over 2 ½ years later. Peter suggested that we "find our pair". He recommended that we learn and specialize in trading only one currency pair for the time being. Every pair has its own characteristics and idiosyncrasies. By focusing on only one pair, Peter felt that we had the best chance to succeed in our trading.

As the morning went on, currency trading was finally making sense to me. Peter's systematic approach to trading was starting to provide the framework that I needed in order to approach trading consistently every day. The logical approach to currency trading that Peter taught made complete sense. These trading concepts are laid out in detail in Peter's "Big Dogs Course".

The candle presentation in the afternoon was as excellent as I expected. Steve Nison explained in great detail the specifics of candles as they applied to the Forex market as the 24-hour nature of this market required some tweaking of the general rules that apply with candles. His presentation focused on how candles send signals about the psychology of the currency markets. Steve spent a lot of time throughout his presentation discussing his "Trading Triad", combining candlestick techniques with Western chart techniques (technical indicators); i.e., looking for confirmation and not just acting on candles alone, along with a strong focus on risk management techniques through the use of candles.

On the flight home, I devoured the written materials from the 'Big Dogs' Course. The 'Big Dogs' Course is several very lengthy and informative books and many hours of very detailed video recordings. Once I was home, I started pouring over the recordings – logging hours toward the 10,000 hour mastery level. I studied these materials for many hours and began trading with these concepts from the Toronto seminar.

In late April, 2008, I received an e-mail from another member of the Forexmentor team. Vic Noble is a full-time currency trader who offers several courses and services to help Forex traders in their trading education and development. Although he had several courses, what interested me was the coaching service he offered—one-on-one meetings by phone and internet for advanced training. In this first email from Vic, there was a link to interviews Vic conducted with successful traders he's worked with at Forexmentor. I listened to these interviews, one after another. In my job, I'm in my car a lot and my wireless internet connection gave me access to many hours of interviews with Vic's successful students. By repetitively reviewing these interviews, I was continuing to log more hours toward the 10,000 hour benchmark.

In my life, I've learned that success leaves clues. I've been taught that, if you want to succeed, find someone who already has succeeded and duplicate their steps to success. Anthony Robbins and others refer to this as modeling. This is why I immediately took advantage of the opportunity to travel to Toronto to learn more about candles from Steve Nison. This is why my two oldest sons work on the psychological side of their golf game with a consultant to the victorious 2008 U.S. Ryder Cup team—to succeed, you work with those who have already succeeded.

Even in this first series of emails with Vic in April, 2008, I could see the level of training and guidance that Forexmentor offers its members. My first questions to Vic concerned entry and exit points on my trades which Vic readily and thoroughly answered for me. In a series of emails over 2 days in late April, I was starting to forge a new friendship with a professional trader and now friend who would soon move me miles down the road toward trading success.

I contacted Vic to request a coaching session. Based on what I heard in the interviews with Vic's students who were experiencing great success, I wanted to jump right into the coaching session and learn from him right away. Vic, however, recommended that

I take my training in a logical progression. First, he recommended that I complete Peter's Big Dogs Course to acquire the general knowledge that I needed to start trading like a professional. Next, he recommended that I consider reviewing his Coach's Guide course to see specifically how he refines the concepts taught in the Big Dogs Course. There was an online course available, but access would have only lasted for six months. The hard copy DVD course would allow me to review this material over and over again which I continue to do almost 3 years later. Repetition and constant review would become a key to my developing the skills and mindset necessary to succeed at trading.

While I started reviewing the new Coach's Guide Course, I also began searching for "my pair" as Peter recommended. I considered volatility, possible price action during my trading hours in the late London to New York sessions and the Asian session along with any personal interests I had in each pair. In considering volatility and price action, I wanted a pair with potential for enough movement each day that it could generate pip action to help me reach my trading goals.

Considering all of these factors, I concluded that the British Pound/U.S. Dollar pair ("Cable" or "Sterling") was the pair that I wanted to study and learn. My only real exposure to this currency was on a golf trip to Northern Ireland in 1995 – I still have some of the British coins as souvenirs from this trip. Without any real knowledge about U.K. economics or Cable's unique characteristics, here's what I did to expedite my learning and shorten the learning curve on my pair.

I mentioned earlier that I used forexfactory.com to find economic announcements that might cause short-term volatility. Now, with a desire to learn my pair, I returned to forexfactory.com with a new attitude – one of using this information and the repeating cycle of economic news to study the impact of the news and, more importantly, the trend of each news item to start to understand where price could be headed on my pair. For example, I learned very quickly that the Purchasing Managers' Index (PMI) announcements the second week of each month were very closely watched. However, only one of the three PMI's was given great weight. The PMI Services number was the much more important of the three data releases because I learned that service jobs constitute approximately 40% of the British economy. While construction and manufacturing were important, they were not the driving force in the economy I was now studying.

I immediately learned the importance of housing statistics. The Halifax, RICS (Royal Institution of Chartered Surveyors) and Nationwide Housing Price Indexes were all being scrutinized for signs of growth or contraction as the U.K. housing industry was a very important segment of the economy.

The Bank of England (BOE), the British Central Bank, regulated interest rates very carefully according to a legal mandate that inflation was the BOE's key factor to control. I sensed very quickly that there was a great deal of pride in the fact that Sterling carried a high rate of interest – there was a very palpable notion that Sterling was an elite currency.

Each month the BOE would announce their interest rate decision followed about two weeks later by the release of the minutes of that month's meeting. The minutes offered a glimpse into the thought process of the Monetary Policy Committee's (MPC) view as to current interest rate levels and where interest rates were headed in the future. If rates were heading higher, investors would eagerly sell the U.S. Dollar and purchase Cable. Rapid movement of 100 pips or more after a rate announcement or the release of MPC minutes were not unusual for the Sterling.

I spent many, many hours online reading The Times of London, The Guardian, and The Telegraph, all British newspapers. I also reviewed www.financialtimes.com to learn about the U.K. economy, sectors of the economy, and the great importance of the banking industry in Britain. I spent many hours on Sunday afternoons and evenings reading the weekend papers to prepare for the trading week ahead. London is a world financial center and is responsible for handling 37% percent of currency transactions compared to only 18% for U.S. banks between April, 2007 and April, 2010. (www.bis.org). Barclays, HSBC, Lloyds, RBS, Blackrock and others became banking names that I followed with great interest. The FTSE, listed on the London Stock Exchange, became a new equity index for me to track as did all worldwide stock exchanges. Through watching and studying worldwide markets and what happened in Sterling price charts day after day, clear patterns of the relationship between price and risk appetite or risk aversion were beginning to show.

Even though the news was not very new by the time I saw it, some expiring airline frequent flier miles provided another invaluable source of learning in the early days of immersing my mind in Cable. A several month subscription to the Financial Times paper provided countless hours of reading material and an opportunity to obtain a real feel for the thoughts and attitudes in the British and European economies. For months, this thick salmon-colored paper in my mailbox provided crucial insight and helped me get up to speed very quickly on news that might affect Sterling.

Deliberate chart time was also critical to learning about the flow and movement of my new pair. Every currency pair has a personality and Sterling has hers. I saw how price reacted very predictably at certain price levels. It was very common to see reactions at the price levels of 20, 50, 80, and "the figure" – 00s (e.g., 1.5720, 1.5750, 1.5780 and 1.5800). The banks and institutional traders had a pattern of driving price to these specific levels and then how they would act once they were there. This was information that could only be acquired through spending time looking at charts, observing price action again and again, watching price throughout the day and realizing that there was some predictability as to how price was moving based on price levels and the time of day.

Through studying chart patterns and because of the knowledge I have from studying candles, I began to see certain candle patterns that were significant with Cable. If a candle pattern called an evening star formed at the 50 level after a steady run-up in price in the London session, this signaled an almost certain pullback, in price. Whether driven by profit-taking or exhaustion in the move up in price, this candle pattern consistently provides a selling opportunity with Sterling. I also observed that bullish or bearish rejection candles were very important price direction indicators especially with Sterling. This pair has the potential to reverse in price dramatically within minutes and rejection candles often signal that impending reversal.

Through enough chart time, I realized another important fact about price moves with Sterling. In technical analysis, there is a tool called fibonacci retracements and extensions. This analysis tool is named after Leonardo Fibonacci, a twelfth-century Italian mathematician. Fibonacci discovered that certain ratios are present in both nature and in mathematical calculations. These ratios are extremely helpful in determining where price may pull back to after a price surge occurs or where price gains may stall.

(For an excellent examination of Fibonacci principles including many chart examples, please review Fibonacci Analysis by Constance Brown, Bloomberg Press, 2008 and Fibonacci for Forex Trading articles by Dick Thompson at www.forexmentor.com). Almost all stock and other trading software includes Fibonacci analysis tools. According to the ratios that Fibonacci discovered, the most common retracement levels or percentages are 38%, 50%, 61.8%, and 79%. For whatever reason, Sterling charts showed me that it was very often a 50% Fibonacci level currency. After a retracement of only 50% with Sterling, and not the typical 61.8% or 79% that other currencies would retrace, Sterling would resume moving again in the direction of the original move it was retracing. Armed with this additional piece of information, I was again adding to my knowledge bank on my pair.

Something else that Peter recommended in Toronto was the need to always have a sandbox to play in, i.e., somewhere to practice new trading ideas safely. At the time of the Toronto seminar, the only option available was a demo account, where I had started my currency trading journey. I followed Peter's suggestion and took this opportunity to test several new demo accounts from different Forex brokers. I learned very quickly which platforms and functions were appealing and which ones were complete turnoffs. I also used these demo trials to test customer service. I found that if a representative couldn't easily answer questions or explain platform features, then there was no reason to consider opening a trading account with them. Since I began training in 2007, brokers have now developed micro accounts where gains and losses are so minimal that the money isn't even an issue. With a micro account, a trader can experience live trading with minimal capital exposure. Having a little money on the line though allows important trading emotions to come into play and makes the trade much more realistic.

Coaching Session — Learning the three steps necessary to dramatically reverse course and trade more consistently

By July, 2008, after finishing my review of the Big Dogs Course and several reviews of the Coach's Guide, and beginning to focus my trading on the Pound/Dollar, it was time for some intensive one-on-one training. The coaching session lasted about 1 ½ hours, but provided many hours, weeks and years worth of information. This information really turned my trading around immediately. Vic stressed the importance of having a consistent approach to the market each day, in how I executed trades and how I managed risk. Regardless of what trade set-up I wanted to look for each day, the key was to trade based on support and resistance levels on higher timeframes. In other words, no more 5-minute chart review for trade entries.

One of the first things we did was to strip my charts of all of the colored lines, bars and indicators that had cluttered my charts (and my mind) for far too long. Without indicators and oscillators all over the charts, the focus was now on price—the only indicator without any time delay or time lag. Vic teaches that price is the ultimate indicator and the concept of "market flow" was all I needed to determine the trend which dictates how to trade each day. Finally, one of the most important pieces of information we discussed was how to manage a trade to reduce risk and to take profits. Vic provided me with numerous pages of chart examples to review to reinforce what we discussed (more hours toward mastery).

Immediately after the coaching session, I joined Vic's Coach's Corner. Coach's Corner was a classroom-type setting where traders from around the world meet twice each week to learn and reinforce the trading principles that Vic teaches. Now it was time to apply that information to my trading.

The World Meltdown — How my new approach to trading immediately paid off even in the face of unimaginable worldwide financial challenges

The world trading environment at the time that I had my coaching session was changing very dramatically. For the week of July 23, 2008, the British Pound reached a high of 2.0076 and closed at 1.9886. The Pound reached its 2008 high of 2.0398 in February, 2008. Its average daily range, the number of pips price moved each day on average from its low to its high was 147 as of July 23, 2008. The prior week of July 13, 2008, the Euro hit a high of 1.6038 and the Australian dollar peaked at .9849. The USD/Yen topped out at 110.68 the week of August 10, 2008.

In the seventeen trading days after my coaching session, the Pound had increased in price only four days. It reached a low of 1.8511 on August 15, 2008. Some daily declines were as much as 300 or more pips, an incredibly unusual move with an average daily range of 147 pips only 2 ½ weeks earlier. On January 23, 2009, six months after my coaching session, Cable closed at 1.3804—a decline of 6188 pips— the world was changing very quickly. The Australian dollar had hit a low of .6547 in November, 2008, the Euro was below 1.2850, and the USD/Yen reached a low of 87.12 in January, 2009. The Dow Jones Industrial average had plunged from 14,093 in October, 2007, to 8852 by October, 2008. Between October, 2007 and October, 2008, the S&P 500 lost 40% and the FTSE fell from 6730 to 4063 (-40%) while the

Nikkei bled from 18,238 in July, 2007, to a dismal 8,693 in October, 2008 (-53%). Oil topped $147.00 a barrel in July, 2008; it plummeted to below $70 per barrel by November, 2008. Bear Stearns disappeared almost overnight in March, 2008; Lehman Brothers filed for bankruptcy in September, 2008, and fears of the total collapse of the world financial system were a daily concern. In this environment of selling all risk assets, it was exceptionally easy to find qualified trade setups to sell the Pound.

I started many days at 4:00 a.m. Eastern ready to act on the latest U.K. economic news releases which were almost always very disappointing. After each news release with worse than expected news, Cable would once again start another red day in earnest. It was very routine to see 100 to 150 pip declines in Cable after each 4:30 a.m. Eastern news announcement. Contrary to my prior economic trading in front of the always good economic news, I was now waiting for confirmation of bad news before pulling the trigger. Several mornings each week, this was an easy trade in this type of historic market environment. As shown in *Figure 8* (end of the book), the Bank of England was slashing interest rates as fast as possible to try to keep up with the spiraling decline of the U.K. economy. There appeared to be a great reluctance to do so initially as Sterling was an "elite" currency. As the economic news quickly worsened and Britain slipped into a recession, the Bank finally had to swallow some pride and join the race with other central banks to near zero interest rate policies followed then by flooding their markets with extra cash to try to alleviate liquidity issues.

Price movements in Cable were so volatile at this time that it was very possible to enter qualified trades two or three times each day from early morning until the Asian session at night. On one day, in particular, prices moved so fast on the Pound that I was able to enter two trades and close out both trades very profitably just during the course of watching my sons play in a golf tournament for several hours. The first trade began and finished on the first nine holes. I then quickly checked charts, ran Fibonacci retracements, looked for my supporting confluences and placed trades. After the second nine holes, I found that, not only had my orders to sell filled after price retraced, but the trade also reached its profit target before the end of the golf tournament!

This propensity to sell the Pound has continued to dominate my approach to trading this currency even after the economic crisis subsided. The several year habit of selling rallies and the extremely high success rate of this approach always leads me to look for signs of weakness in a Cable rally. After spending many hours of watching price action at varying price levels, I've learned that Cable will usually respect a significant price support or resistance level the first time price gets back to that point, especially if it's one of the "magic numbers" for Cable—20, 50, 80 or 00. Using the entry techniques I learned in the Coach's Guide and in my coaching session, there are often many possible trades at these levels.

Driving Trades — The clear benefits of analyzing a trade and then using driving as a way to manage the trade

With five boys ages 9-19 who are very active in sports and with a job that requires some travel most weeks, there are many days where I'm not able to sit in front of a desktop computer. With a laptop and a wireless connection, and more recently, with a cell phone, I've found several ways to stay in touch with the markets. Many of my trades are, of necessity, driving trades. In the early stages of my trading, those 5 minute chart days, I definitely had too much access to the markets. One click trading made it too easy to enter trades at times. As I finally settled down to focus on one predominant currency and only a few trade set-ups based on higher time frame support and resistance concepts, the wireless capability is now used to monitor trades and not just initiate trades based on random decision-making. Many of my most profitable (and least stressful) trades over the last few years have been initiated with limit orders set early in the morning which I may or may not be able to monitor during the day when I'm on the road. Depending on the strength of my wireless internet connection, in certain areas where I may travel during the week or on the weekend, I do not have access to the internet on my laptop. In many situations, that's turned out to be the best trade monitoring scenario.

Without the opportunity to watch every price hiccup and gyration, there's no chance to second guess profit targets and over-manage a trade. Currency prices generally do not move up or down in a straight line. Instead, they move one direction, consolidate, may pullback, move some more, spike, consolidate, rise or fall rapidly and continue this never-ending and unpredictable rollercoaster ride. Compared to often erratic 5 and 15 minutes charts, 1 hour and 4 hour charts for the same time period may appear very calm.

At times, being able to move stops and manage trades is beneficial. However, *Figures 9-13* (back of the book), are charts from some of my "driving trades" over the last 2 years which clearly show why the best trade management plan is sometimes to go on the road as I've done with these trades. These were not scalp trades where minute-by-minute attention is necessary for management of the trade. With the longer-term,

---

bigger move trades illustrated in these charts, price needs time to make its move toward the intended target. Once the risk is taken out of the trade, and some profit is taken, there's nothing to do but to go for a drive and wait—it's worked many, many times for me!

The Ultimate Road Trip — Balancing family and trading; logging learning hours the hard way

There were no trades on this road trip, but this illustrates the lengths that I'll go to in order to put myself in a position to be around the successful people who can teach me and help me get closer to the 10,000 hour mark. For several weeks in spring, 2009, I received e-mails regarding a weekend seminar which Chris Lori was hosting in Charlotte, North Carolina. Chris doesn't hold many live seminars each year. The only other seminar scheduled that year was going to be in New Zealand, which was not a very good option for me. I had heard Chris on several internet webinars and always found his presentations and the information he discussed to be extremely insightful, very timely, and immediately useful in my trading. Chris has a background as a former Olympic athlete for Canada (4 Olympic Games). He was a member of Canada's Championship

World Cup Bobsled Team (22 World Cup Medals), so he understands the principles of persistence, discipline, and dedication. (See Amazon.com for Chris' book Fiercely Driven about his bobsledding career). Chris' athletic disciplines have certainly contributed to tremendous success in currency trading. Chris is now a CTA and fund manager for individuals and institutions. With his success in world-level bobsledding and his in-depth knowledge of currency trading, institutional trading issues, and psychological trading issues, this was a weekend that I did not want to miss. However, that same weekend was also the weekend of the Senior Prom. My oldest son would be heading for college in a few months and I wanted to be a part of my son's prom that weekend.

Here's how I dealt with that dilemma. Nashville is 425 miles from Charlotte. I attended Chris' seminar on Friday afternoon where he covered the basics of how he trades currencies professionally. Saturday morning, after about half an hour in the seminar, it was time for the road. I timed my trip to my home to arrive for Prom pictures and to see my son, his date, and their friends off to dinner. Then it was back in the car to head back to Charlotte. During the ten plus hour road trip that day, I listened to recordings of Chris' Pro Traders Club (PTC) presentations. PTC presentations are released several times each week with a review of price action, chart patterns and Chris' thoughts on currency trends. Chris or his guests always discussed the trade setups which Chris teaches, what price action actually did, and how Chris or the guests handled each trade. Each PTC is an excellent learning opportunity. Even though I missed the Saturday seminar and couldn't watch the charts being reviewed in the PTC talks, by listening to these recordings for many hours, I was learning Chris' trading methods and becoming a better trader, both technically and psychologically.

I arrived back in Charlotte after 1:00 a.m. Eastern on Sunday morning. Getting to sleep was not a problem at all. Even with missing the actual seminar on Saturday, I spent the better part of two days live with Chris and one day on the road with Chris learning the chart patterns he trades, how he manages trades and learning his philosophy toward trading. The hours were starting to accumulate.

IV. Forexmentor's Big Step Forward

Consistently profitable trading made available on a daily basis

In June, 2009, Forexmentor's commitment to their mission of training currency traders worldwide to be consistently profitable became very evident. Coach's Corner, a twice a week live coaching program hosted by Vic Noble had been, and continues to be, an incredible educational training resource. Coach's Corner was expanded to include a daily live training component where traders and coaches can interact real time throughout the trading session. They called this new expanded service "Forexmentor LiveConnect." Forexmentor LiveConnect (LC) was launched to assist traders in focusing on:

1. How they approach trading each day;
2. Risk management in trades; and,
3. Improving consistency in trade management.

Beginning in the early hours of the day before the London market opens at 2:00 a.m. Eastern, a daily video preview of the London market session (7-10 minutes) is posted for members to review. Members are alerted of the price levels to watch for, major areas of support and resistance to pay attention to, current trends of the major currencies, possible trade setups, and a review of economic news for the day are among the many topics covered in each preview video. At least one, and more often than not, two "moderators" are present in the LC room to answer questions, review price movement, discuss possible new trade set-ups, and provide coaching for new and experienced traders alike. The moderators are very successful traders; some even trade professionally for their own clients. Discussions are conducted by interactive chat with the ability at any time for a moderator to turn on a microphone and review price charts and go over any questions from LC members.

Don't like to or can't trade in the early morning hours or in the middle of the night? No problem. LC moderators also post a pre-New York video around 8:00 a.m. Eastern to review price action for the day so far, the current status of LC set-ups being watched, New York session economic news events, and other issues that could impact trading action.

The resources that are available in the LC room very quickly help members move down the road toward the 10,000 hour mastery figure.

These resources include the pre-London and pre-New York videos, an extensive video library of trade set-ups taught in LC, an archive of hundreds of hours of actual trades (from the start of LC in June, 2009 until the present) recordings of the spur of the moment chart reviews by the moderators, videos on weekly trade reviews and video tutorials on various indicators such as pivots, fractals, MT4, and E-Signal and an ADR calculator among others.

These resources and the ability to learn from and ask questions of professional traders, the moderators and other successful LC traders every day is so very important. This is the exact opposite of what I experienced when I began trading currencies. Learning comes very rapidly with these resources (or "opportunities" as Gladwell calls them in Outliers).

Looking back now, all of this information potentially posed a challenge for me. As I'll discuss in detail in section VI of this book on trading resources, too much information can be distracting for my personality. I tend to make decisions very impulsively at times; always have and probably always will. The constant flow of information about possible trade set-ups on an intraday basis on many currency pairs did overwhelm me at first. I found myself face-to-face with one of the biggest trading barriers that I would have to conquer in order to succeed at trading – the fear of missing a move, as I call it. Knowing that there was a qualified set-up or that there might be some qualified set-ups each day in LC that I might miss with my busy schedule every day with work and my family frustrated me at times. With all of this information, I had to fight from losing my focus at times. My impatient personality would get the best of me some days. I was taking trades without a real comfort level for a currency pair and without having done the background work necessary to know support and resistance levels or even just key price levels on that pair.

From June, 2009 until December, 2009, I continued to learn from the LC moderators and members and from the Coach's Corner meetings each week. The investment risk environment had turned around completely from the free fall days that began in October, 2007. Equity markets bottomed in March, 2009 and were continuing to retrace their staggering losses. Currency trading was not so one-sided any more.

During the summers, my trading activities slow down as I travel a lot with vacations and attending golf tournaments with two of my sons. We have some great times each summer travelling together. Trading is generally slower in the summer months anyway. Activity tends to pick up sometime after the Labor Day holiday in the United States. Trading activity then races toward the end of the year and slows down again in December as institutional traders lock in profits and close the books on the year. With the New Year on the horizon, it was time to think about and plan the next step in my trading. It was time to set goals and refocus my trading efforts.

V. The Start of the 7 Day Plan

How committing to develop myself revolutionized my life and my trading

"Welcome all experiences. You never know which one is going to turn everything on." Jim Rohn

Over fifteen years ago, I was involved in a home-based business with Rexall, a well-respected name in the United States for the 100-year old corner drugstores. The Rexall home-based company specialized in marketing nutritional products that focused on preventative health. Although having long ceased to be actively involved in that business, my family and I continue to benefit from my involvement many years ago. My wife and I celebrated our 25th anniversary in 2010. In early 2010, she was diagnosed with diabetes. Because of my involvement with the Rexall business fifteen years ago, I had learned of a natural product they distributed which, as confirmed by a double blind clinical trial at The Cleveland Clinic in Cleveland, Ohio, was effective in reducing blood sugar. I had personally witnessed people with a long history of diabetes who were able to dramatically reduce their blood sugar levels. Through exercise, diet changes and the use of this natural product, my wife lowered her blood sugar from over 200 when she was diagnosed to readings that are consistently below 110. Even though my Rexall business was not a financial success, the current health benefit for my wife from this product is certainly more than enough for us to say that our experience with Rexall over fifteen years ago was worth the time and effort. Aside from this tremendous health benefit that my wife's experiencing now, I'm currently in the middle of receiving many more benefits from that time in Rexall in the 1990s.

While attending a series of meetings in California over fifteen years ago to learn from doctors and other experts about the Rexall products, one of the speakers focused on setting and achieving goals. Fortunately, I purchased a book that the speaker Bob Davies wrote called The Sky Is Not the Limit, You Are! (Carlsbad, In-Fact Publishing Co., 1994). Bob Davies had a very successful background in coaching and helping sports teams and individuals as well as business leaders in setting goals and learning how to accomplish those goals.

In December, 2009, as I started to think about my trading in 2009 and my somewhat inconsistent results at times, and to focus on my goals for the new year, I ran across Bob Davies' book and read it again. It had been over fifteen years since I last opened the pages of this book, but it was about to change the course of my trading and my life forever. I have set goals in the past, written them down, and reviewed them frequently as other programs teach, but toward the end of the book, I ran across the concept that started what is now called "The 7 Day Plan" in the Monday Coach's Corner meetings. Bob teaches that accomplishing goals only occurs from creating leverage with external and internal support and accountability. The external support comes from having a partner along the lines of the "Master Mind" principle from Think and Grow Rich (New York: Ballantine Books, 1960). According to Bob:

> *Practice has shown that a master mind group will accomplish much more than any one of them could do individually....You can more easily create positive results in your life when you are open to looking at yourself, your problems and your opportunities from another's point of view. Another way of saying this is to have coaching in your life.... When someone else holds*

*you to as high or higher an expectation than you hold yourself,
breakthroughs occur. Davies, Sky Is Not The Limit, pgs. 82-83.*

Bob Davies went on to say that "By being held accountable to do a specific activity it changes what paradigms I see. I see opportunities to perform, rather than reasons why I can't." (Sky, pg. 89)

Inspired by these thoughts, I e-mailed Vic Noble and told him about my desire to start this partnering and accountability approach to my trading in 2010. I told Vic in an e-mail of December 13, 2009, about the 7 day goal setting plan that Bob Davies recommends with a system of $5.00 fines when a goal is not accomplished in this plan. Not having a plan in place for the next week results in a $20.00 fine. I then spelled out in detail my plans for the next week for the setups I was looking for, how I would look for these setups, how I would manage these trades, and my plans for personal development activities and physical fitness goals.

Excited by the proposal, Vic immediately agreed to serve as my accountability partner. Vic told me that he thought that "being accountable is one of the more over-looked aspects of traders. After all, who's going to know if you screw up? By taking an honest, more "public" approach like this, it serves as a great way to hold your own feet to the fire." Fines for violations of my trading plan or not accomplishing any of my 7 day goals were to be donated to local charities such as children's hospitals. The first 7 Day Plan called for me to limit my trading to Cable on three specific trade setups. I set goals for workouts and sleep each night so that I had the physical and mental energy I needed each day. I spelled out what tapes I would listen to in my car on personal development, that I would start re-reading "Trading in the Zone" by Mark

Douglas, and that I would review an internet webinar on trading psychology by Chris Lori. One week later, I followed up with this report:

I had traded only the set-ups I was looking for and managed them as planned; listened to tapes and read Zone as planned except for one set of tapes; started review of Lori and Nison webinars; worked out as planned, but missed the sleep I wanted on 2 nights. I spelled out the trade plan for the next week as well as plans for managing trades and personal development materials that I would review.

So, the 7 Day Plan was launched. Since that first e-mail, I have continued to plan my week in advance according to the daily activities that I need to engage in to reach my trading and life goals. As a result of the 7 Day Plan, I have become more focused on my short, medium, and long-term goals; begun to achieve more balance in my life; achieved more consistent trading results; improved my physical fitness; and have spent countless hours reviewing personal development materials.

As Jim Rohn so strongly advises, "work harder on yourself than you do on your job." I continue to send reports to Vic at the beginning of the week to discuss what was and was not accomplished the prior week in the areas of exercise, trading, family time, and personal and psychological development. Working on goals daily in this manner has helped me build momentum toward my goals.

Throughout the 7 day process, I have spent many hours on acquiring knowledge and experience not just about the technical side of trading. Looking back over the last year, the most beneficial use of my time with the 7 Day Plan has been the many hours I've spent daily and weekly on improving and sharpening the psychological side of my trading. In the next section of this book, I'll describe in detail the resources which

I have found to be extremely important and beneficial in helping me move along the road to the 10,000 hour milestone. These resources include some trading resources, but primarily contain personal development resources that focus on the psychological side of trading. The combination of these resources has helped me to overcome many early trading roadblocks, obstacles and erroneous beliefs.

After discussing the trading and personal development resources that have benefited me the most in the last year, I'll then spell out some ideas on how anyone can start and follow their own 7 Day Plan.

VI. Personal and Trading Development Resources

Since the beginning of the 7 Day Plan, my focus has been on daily accountability for my trading and personal development. For over one year, the books, tapes, webinars, CDs and DVDs that I've reviewed have reshaped or reinforced my trading and life skills.

The resources that I am about to discuss are by no means the only resources that will improve your trading skills and psychological development as a trader. However, some of these materials, regardless of what financial instrument you trade, definitely should become part of your trading library. As you'll see throughout this section, many times it was a combination of materials, an adaptation of or modification of an idea, with lots of repetition, that impacted me the most. Constant review of these materials and combining or adapting some of these ideas have lead to some very significant breakthroughs for me in the past twelve months. Your challenge in your personal development quest is to determine what information you need to review in order to improve your technical skills as a trader and, probably more importantly, how you can improve your approach to trading from a psychological point of view.

The Zone — Acquiring the correct trading attitudes that will promptly change your view of trading

After first learning about Forexmentor in Toronto in April, 2008, you'll recall that I started receiving emails from Vic Noble regarding his interviews with very successful traders that he's coached. Again and again, I heard these traders mystically refer to a book—"The Zone"—Trading In the Zone by Mark Douglas (New York: Prentice Hall Press, 2000). Success leaves clues—I bought the book immediately.

The Zone begins with a short quiz to determine a trader's current mental attitudes toward trading. When I read the book the first time in May, 2008, I learned that I wanted every trade set-up to be a winner. I also found that I was not trading based on probability and, if a trade was a loser, I was convinced it was because I didn't know enough about the markets. In particular, I believed that it was because I didn't know enough about the technical side of trading such as the particular application of certain indicators on my charts. Several days later when I finished the book, I realized how completely wrong my mindset was on trading.

The Zone focuses on the probabilities inherent in trading and the correct mental attitudes that successful traders carry in their trading.

I've now read this book several times since I bought it over two years ago.

I've just completed another complete re-read of the book in January and February, 2011. Every time I read the book, I learn something new about trading and myself as a trader, because I'm at a new point in my maturity as a trader. The information in this book is vitally important to your success as a trader—this is the first book to buy to start your trading library.

By breaking down all of the emotions that come with trading into a logical sequence of explanations, this book will very quickly point out areas where a trader needs improvement—e.g., attitudes toward trading; accountability and responsibility for wins and losses; the neutrality of the market and price; and the role of beliefs and perceptions that a trader may have and how they impact trading decisions.

One of the most important parts of the book is how Mark Douglas clearly spells out the seven essential elements necessary to create the belief that a trader is a "consistent winner." This is a list to post by your computer where you trade, in your car on the dashboard, on your bathroom mirror and on your night stand—carrying a copy in your pocket to review throughout the day is a great idea too. The book concludes with a trading exercise which will firmly instill these seven trading keys into a trader's belief system. This exercise will lead to trading actions based on these keys.

At the end of the book, you will take the same trading quiz that started the book— your new answers will be very surprising. A suggestion; keep all of your quiz answers from each time you read the book. Over time, you'll see remarkable changes in your trading attitudes and beliefs as you mature as a trader.

Visualization — The power of using your mind to direct your trading

There are many personal development books, tapes and CDs which make reference to visualizing a goal "in your mind's eye" or in "the theatre in your mind". This concept is frequently credited to Dr. Maxwell Maltz in another must have book for your trading library—The New Psycho-Cybernetics (New York: Prentice Hall Press, 2001). As a plastic surgeon, Dr. Maltz discovered that the work he performed on the outside of the body would not be successful if the internal picture a patient held of themselves was in conflict. Dr. Maltz concluded that your self-image "controls what you can and cannot accomplish." More importantly, he found that "all actions,

feelings, behavior, even your abilities, are always consistent with this self-image."
Psycho-Cybernetics, p.3.

Reading this landmark book may help you break through any fears, such as fear of failure or of success, which may be adversely impacting your trading results. Dr. Maltz's "Mental Training Exercises" throughout the book systematically take the reader through all issues of self-image, beliefs and habits which could be negatively dragging down your trading account balance.

One of the most important training exercises in the book is the practice of visualization. Through the repetitive, sensory rich practice of imagining the intended results of your goals, the self-image (the subconscious) will believe that these images are real. This is the technique that world-class athletes use to achieve their success. The self-image is rebuilt or reprogrammed over time with this practice. The key to visualization practice is to fill your practice sessions with such vivid detail that it absolutely feels real to the subconscious.

I have loved the game of golf for many years. My family spends many hours on the golf course. I've mentioned that one of my sons now plays college golf. In the past, I've used visualization to improve my golf shots. I've spent time before a round of golf imagining a particular shot that I knew I would have to hit later that day. When it came time to hit that shot, there have been many occasions where I would picture the shot that I've already hit on the range, tell myself confidently that "I've already hit this shot" and then do it. The results were very, very good sometimes. I've used audiotapes in the past designed for golfers that involved visualization practice which I knew helped my game, so I completely understood Dr. Maltz's principles and conclusions on how important visualization is in my trading.

In my trading visualization practice, I use all of the senses as Dr. Maltz directs. If I'm visualizing the start of the trading day, I make breakfast—feel, see and hear the dishes; smell and hear the food cooking and how the dishes feel in my hands as I walk to my office. I feel the floor under my feet, see the rooms in my house in the light conditions for that part of the day (usually very dark!). Once I'm looking at price charts, I see the colors of the candles and use current price levels for the pairs I'm reviewing. I review the different time frames starting with the daily and then work my way lower, I see the support/resistance levels marked on my charts, I review MACD and slow stochastic indicators (that's all now). I see my desk, how it looks, what books are on my desk, and other parts of my office. I see the orders I'm placing, the stop level, and the different levels where I'll take profits. I visualize risk management as I calculate what orders I will place, (I see my account balance growing each time I practice), visualize the orders filling, watch price move after entry, take profits at the amount of my stop, see and hear price alarms going off to alert me to move stops to reduce risk or to lock in profits. I watch price, pivots, support and resistance levels on 15 minute and 1 hour charts to know when to move my stops. I see portions of the trade close out for profits at pre-set profit levels,

I see the tab on my trading platform start to show "Closed Positions", and I feel the sense of accomplishment that comes with a winning trade.

At times, I'll imagine a news development which affects my trade, the stock market numbers and how they are developing during the trade, what time it is—is it time to take some more profits off if selling or buying is about to slow for the day? Once the trade is over—the best part—filling out the check request form to fax to my broker. I fill out each line of the form in detail in my mind. Even better, I visualize going to the mailbox a few days later and opening the envelope with the check with my name on it—how does the envelope look, feel, what color is the check and what are the numbers to the right of my name? The check of course must go to the bank—I take a drive, see things along the way, walk into the bank, talk with the teller and finally feel the deposit slip in my hand. Through all of these many detailed activities, I'm doing everything possible to make the experience very real for the subconscious. Sometimes price moves fast, sometimes it consolidates for a while, or moves then retraces—I imagine all of the different scenarios.

You can see from this description that I've taken Dr. Maltz's teaching to heart. On longer term trades, such as a 4 hour chart trade, I've seen that price may actually move very much in line with what I've already visualized ("I've already hit this shot"). Having already experienced the event in my mind, it's very easy to handle managing the trade when it comes along.

Suggested Action Plan:

Buy Dr. Maltz's book or the tapes. (I found an old set of the tapes with recordings of Dr. Maltz's lectures in a used book store for $3.00.) Practice the visualization techniques he spells out. This is something that will improve with each practice; try to increase the details every time you practice.

Jim Rohn: "Work Harder on Yourself than you do on your Job" — Why you need to develop your own personal philosophy and how that decision changes your life

This statement really epitomizes what I've done since December, 2009 with the 7 Day Plan. I've spent some time tweaking and refining how I manage my trades and my trade selection. At one point, my trading platform had one lonely currency on it—the British Pound. Although my platform has other currencies showing on it again, my focus in my chart review and trading is exclusively centered on the British Pound again.

However, the vast amount of time I spend each week is working on myself. Whether I'm working on physical fitness; reviewing my short, medium and long-term goals; reading books and taking notes; listening to tapes or CD's in my car or working on visualization practice, working very hard on me is the focus of the 7 Day Plan.

A quick look at www.jimrohn.com (Celebrating the Life and Legacy of Jim Rohn-Full Event Video) very quickly shows just how highly Jim was thought of in the personal development arena (Jim passed away in December, 2009). This video showcases some of the biggest names in personal development and public speaking who came together for Jim's Memorial service in February, 2010. Reviewing this 2 hour video is a terrific use of your time at night or on the weekend. Here's a partial list of some of the people who paid tribute to Jim and what they said: Brian Tracy: "He taught the American dream. You can start with nothing, but you can make it to the top if you'll do certain things: Set goals, take notes, accept responsibility and take action"; Anthony Robbins (had to scrape up $35.00 from his part-time janitor job in high school when he was 17 to attend his first Jim Rohn seminar. He ended up working for Jim the next 3 years and attended 32 seminars in that time.): Jim "gave in ways others don't give". "I am inspired every day because of Jim"; Mark Victor Hansen: Jim Rohn was "one of the great and inspiring teachers…of our time and probably all time.". Zig Ziglar; John C. Maxwell; Dennis Waitley ("Earl Nightingale called Jim the greatest business philosopher of all time.") and Harvey Mackay were among the many people who paid tribute to Jim and to his ability to teach, coach, inspire and mentor millions of people around the world on how to reach their potential in business and in life.

Among Jim Rohn's many books and audio programs, "The Art of Exceptional Living" is absolutely at the top of the list. In this program, Jim discusses his personal life and business philosophies as taught to him by his mentor. Jim's purpose in life was to make a major contribution to the lives of those people he spoke to through his books, audio programs or live seminars. The Jim Rohn Memorial service on his website shows that Jim did just that many times over. After you watch this Memorial service, you will understand the importance of committing to lifelong personal development.

I've reviewed Exceptional Living repeatedly in the last year— sometimes several times in the same week. I have sections of the tapes memorized now. Why listen repetitively? Per Jim: "To continue to expose yourself to the ideas that can make a dramatic difference in your life—you don't know when they will come into play." More importantly, every time you hear an idea, that may be the right time in your life for that idea to significantly change your life. Why take notes on meetings, books, audio programs, webinars or seminars? "To capture the ideas that inspire you--don't trust your memory." Jim advises. More importantly, in order to build a library of your journals of the important ideas that affected your life—one of the 3 important legacies to leave about your life. Based on Jim's advice, I've started building my library of journals.

The Art of Exceptional Living clearly spells out Jim's attitudes on issues such as the fundamentals of life; success and failure; self-discipline; reading, learning and personal development ("for things to change, you have to change"; "if you will change, things will change for you"). Jim also discusses what success really is in life; lifestyle, setting and reaching goals, and financial independence among the many, many topics covered in this audio program. Unlike some audio programs, this one ends too quickly. I developed my short-term, 1 year, 3 year, 5 year and 10 year goals based on what Jim Rohn teaches in this program. As Jim was so fond of saying, "It's not what you get in life, it's what you become."

Suggested Action Plan:

Sign up for Jim's newsletter on www.jimrohn.com. Each newsletter contains an article from Jim Rohn and articles from other personal success icons. Add The Art of Exceptional Living to your library. Review it at least once per month, take detailed notes, review those notes frequently and implement the steps to success that Jim teaches. Every book, tape, CD or DVD that Jim has put together can change your life if you will study success as Jim teaches.

Bob Proctor — The value of continuous learning for the rest of your life

I'm always signing up for webinars that involve personal development or psychology of trading issues. As I'm writing this book, the 2010 Money Show Traders Expo is scheduled in Las Vegas. I won't be there in person, but there are over 30 presentations from the program that will be broadcast on the internet. With the internet, there are countless learning opportunities every week.

I've learned from my constant review of personal development materials that Bob Proctor is extremely well thought of for his life-coaching skills. I've reviewed several of his programs for many hours – "The Science of Getting Rich" and "Working with the Law". Both of these audio programs focus on the mental side of success—the attitudes and beliefs that must be followed in business, relationships and all areas of life to excel. The book which Bob discusses in The Science of Getting Rich was the book that prompted Rhonda Byrne to come up with the idea for the ground-breaking movie "The Secret".

One of the most important success principles which Bob constantly discusses is having gratitude in our life. He teaches a simple method of increasing gratitude every day and attracting the goals we've set for ourselves. At Bob Proctor's suggestion, I have a notebook full of pages and pages of the goals I'm working on right now. Each page begins with this simple statement: "I am so happy and grateful now that…" followed by the written goals I've set for myself. These written statements incorporate both gratitude and visualization as they are in the present tense; they've already occurred. If there's a busy time in my day where I can't write another page, I can just read the pages I've already written to further my goal review. Whether read silently or out loud several times a day, I'm continuing to drive these goals into my subconscious. Through various sources, I've seen universal agreement that the subconscious is more receptive to these suggestions the first thing in the morning and right before going to sleep. Therefore, one of the first things I'm doing each morning is to write or re-read "The Proctor List" as I call it. At night, before bed, I'm again flooding my subconscious with these thoughts.

While writing this book, I've discovered another tremendous learning resource which Bob Proctor offers at www.bobproctor.com. Bob offers free weekly teaching calls on Mondays. These calls focus on issues regarding abundance, visualization, portions from must-have personal development books, and attitudes necessary for success. How can these calls be used? The archive of the recordings of these calls, now several years in length, presents another tool for me to use in the early morning if there's not a trading opportunity, if I'm in my car, at lunch, in the evenings, or on the weekends. The possibilities are endless.

For another opportunity, in alignment with Napolean Hill's Think and Grow Rich and the importance of having a master mind group to work together to help others reach their goals, visit www.bobproctormastermindgroups.com. There's no cost to join a master mind group (they are operating all over the world) to receive support and encouragement. This is just a central location which Bob has created to help people all over the world work together to achieve their goals.

Bob Proctor talks about gratitude, as I mentioned, but he does more than talk. He practices giving to others with his weekly calls, daily inspirational messages (sign up at www.bobproctor.com) and free copies of books and articles on his website.

If you don't own a copy of Think and Grow Rich by Napolean Hill, put this book down right now and go order a copy immediately. As with Trading In the Zone and Psycho-Cybernetics, this book should be one of the centerpieces of your trading library. Napolean Hill interviewed multi-millionaire Andrew Carnegie on his secrets of incredible success. Carnegie told Hill that he gained his fortune by learning to control his mind and how he thought. Carnegie challenged Hill to spend 20 years researching and analyzing their discussions to flush out the concepts which Carnegie used first to accumulate his fortune and then to give it all away to charity. To complete this book, Hill analyzed the lives of people such as Henry Ford, Theodore Roosevelt, Wilbur Wright, William Jennings Bryan, John D. Rockefeller, Thomas Edison, Clarence Darrow, Woodrow Wilson, Dr. Alexander Graham Bell, and Charles M. Schwab to determine how they used Carnegie's principles to achieve unbelievable success in their lives.

"Think and Grow Rich" is a book to be read and studied again and again as each reading reveals a new understanding of the twelve steps toward riches which Hill writes about in the book. Some chapters are long and some chapters are short, but every word and each sentence was carefully chosen because of the life-changing wisdom that's involved. How important is "Think and Grow Rich"? Bob Proctor has been studying it for almost 50 years. In one of his conference calls, Bob commented that he is focusing his study on one chapter per month right now. Despite his remarkable financial success, and his reputation for being one of the most inspiring motivational speakers and teachers, Bob continues to improve his personal skills through repetitive review of this book. Success leaves clues. Study "Think and Grow Rich" and learn from Bob Proctor through his website, books and articles.

The Ultimate Visualization Tool — Programing your mind for success in only a few minutes every day

As I mentioned in my discussion of Psycho-Cybernetics, I've had prior experience and success in using visualization while playing golf. I've also observed that when I listen to a book on tape or CD in my car, I can vividly remember exactly where I was the last time I heard a specific portion of a book or statement on a CD. Because I'm so visually oriented, as are the majority of people, I can see the section of the road I was on, the street signs around me, the scenery on the road, and all other details the next time I hear that same portion of the book or CD. I was convinced that if I could find a way to combine my visual orientation with audio, that would be a tremendous tool for me to use to achieve my goals. In summer, 2009, I discovered that tool. I learned that several entrepreneurs from Australia had put together exactly what I was looking for – an easy system of building a personalized visualization "mind movie" (http://www.mindmovies.com/mm21/Manifesting.php?17582). They launched their product only a few years ago and it has exploded worldwide.

I am not at all a techie type person. I still have no idea how to cut and paste e-mails. Learning how to clip an attachment to an e-mail has been my biggest technological achievement in the last two years. However, the Mind Movies system was extremely simple for me to use to put together my own miniature movie of my goals. With recent revisions to their system, (Version 2.0 and Version 2.1 as of April, 2011) it's now even easier to put together a mind movie. A series of short video tutorials walked me through each step and taught me how to write my script, locate pictures, add my inspirational song, and then put everything together into a short five-minute movie that I review every day to drive these goals into my subconscious.

The script writing was very easy – remember the Bob Proctor gratitude list that started with "I am so happy and grateful now that…"? This list formed the core of my script. After adding other goals, I then added pictures of the places around the world where we want to travel as a family, the charities that we want to help, the lifestyle that we will live, and various trading disciplines that I want to make sure that I follow. The song that I chose was a high-energy song that has been my favorite song since I was in college. This is the song that always fired me up whenever I heard it. My day now starts and ends with images filling my subconscious with my goals, dreams, and aspirations – some of which have already been accomplished.

What if I can't be in front of my computer to watch my mind movie? Here's the solution which I created. Tony Robbins discusses the principle of "anchoring" in his many excellent books and audio programs. This is the process of using a specific physical gesture to link any representation to that gesture. Using that concept, I've come up with a physical gesture that I anchor with while I'm watching a certain portion of my mind movie. Through repetition, I can now fire that anchor and then clearly see and hear this specific portion of my mind movie. The pictures and the corresponding script for these pictures are so firmly embedded in my subconscious now that I can call them up with my anchor in only a few seconds. From repetition, I can also now just listen to my mind movies song in my car or even just play the song in my mind and I will see the pictures and written goals in my mind.

A mind movie can be reviewed several times a day or it can be reviewed the entire time you're in front of the computer where it's created.

Mind Movies has a software program called Subliminal Success Accelerator (SSA), which, when installed on your computer, will play your mind movie faintly in the background of your computer screen while you go about your workday on the computer. In the meantime, your subconscious is being reminded of the goals you've set for yourself.

Very recently, I learned a really fantastic piece of advice from Natalie Ledwell, one of Mind Movies' developers. Because I'm always on the lookout for interviews with successful people, I recently learned that Natalie was speaking about the Mind Movies story and how they became so successful. In the interview, Natalie said that she practiced gratitude by journaling five things that she was grateful for each day just before she went to bed. Gratitude attracts more to be grateful for, of course. However, one of the rules of this exercise is that each day has to have five new gratitude items. This forces you to be on the lookout for all there is to truly be grateful for each day. Why at night? Because the subconscious is extremely receptive to ideas and suggestions such as gratitude before going to sleep while the theta brain waves are beginning to form. When the brain is in the theta wave stage, healing, learning and growth occur. The subconscious is very easy to access through theta waves which also occur in the first 5-15 minutes after waking up each day—the perfect time to access the mind with visualization practice.

Not being able to repeat gratitude items from prior days has forced me to really be alert to all of the many blessings which I have in my life. If I approach each day on the lookout for the people, events, and blessings which I should truly appreciate, I'm finding that this is a remarkable way to live each day.

As a digital visualization tool, Mind Movies helps me stay focused on my goals. If repetition is the first law of learning, then combining repetition with strong emotions from Mind Movie images is an incredibly successful method of reaching the subconscious.

Suggested Action Plan

Maxwell Maltz wrote an entire book on the critical importance of visualization. Mindmovies.com presents the vehicle to make visualization a very convenient and successful process. Repetitive review of your mind movie will put your subconscious to work on your goals. With your sub-conscious acting on your goals every day, it must take steps to attract what you want to have, be and do -- much easier and much faster. Mind Movies Version 2.1: http://www.mindmovies.com/mm21/Manifesting.php?17582

Brett Steenbarger — How to discover any barriers that limit your trading results

In the area of trading psychology, Brett Steenbarger is extremely well-respected. Dr. Steenbarger has been a Professor of Psychology at the State University of New York (SUNY). At SUNY, he taught the medical students and also ran a clinical practice for the medical students and the faculty. He now works with Kingstree Trading, LLC, a trader's training and research organization. Dr. Steenbarger has written many thousands of pages of articles on trading psychology which are available at no charge on his web site www.brettsteenbarger.com. His books, The Psychology of Trading, Enhancing Trader Performance (Hoboken: John Wiley and Sons, Inc., 2007) and The Daily Coach: 101 Lessons for Becoming Your Own Trading Psychologist (Hoboken: John Wiley and Sons, Inc., 2009), together with other books are highly recommended.

My first experience with Dr. Steenbarger came from a DVD recording of a trading seminar in Las Vegas several years ago. I've listened to Trader's Guide to Self-Discipline: Techniques for Changing Emotional Patterns (www.traderslibrary.com) many, many times while I've been driving. As with all self-development materials, repetition, careful thought and reflection lead to a new understanding and appreciation of the personal development information each time it's reviewed—that's especially true for me with Dr. Steenbarger's materials.

After listening to the DVD in my car many times and watching it at night and taking several sets of notes, I finally found the key to unlocking the mysteries of my trading behaviors which have held me back at times, especially in the early days of trading currencies. Through his clinical practice and his work with traders, Dr. Steenbarger has learned that many unwanted, detrimental trading behaviors are the result of a "vertical split."

This personality split is the outward representation of the person we don't want to be—the alien trader that will occasionally invade our minds before, during or after a trade. Vertical splits will make it very difficult to maintain consistency. Without a vertical split, consistency and controlled trading occurs. With a split, inconsistent and unexplainable trading behavior and decisions occur.

The split occurs because of the way that the brain codes our emotionally organized behaviors. According to his research, Dr. Steenbarger determined that the brain stores non-emotional behavior patterns such as concentration and focus in the frontal lobe. Emotionally charged behaviors and events are stored in the right hemisphere and lower areas of the brain.

In his DVD presentation, Dr. Steenbarger describes how a "trade trigger" activates the right hemisphere and lower lobe stored emotions. These emotions then cause decisions in trading that, at times, would lead me to ask post-trade questions such as "why in the world did I enter that trade where I did", "what was I thinking when I placed that trade order" or "why did I manage my trade that way"? Typical trading behaviors that trade triggers set off include under-controlled trading (over trading, adding to a losing position and not moving stops to lock in profits/reduce risk in a trade) and over-controlled trading (not being patient and letting the trade play out and run to the desired profit target).

After hearing these statements repeatedly, after taking several sets of notes, and after a lot of thought, I discovered that, because of my tendency to make impulsive (under-controlled) decisions at times in my life, many of my trading errors occurred because of these trade triggers:

1. My Concern that I might "miss a move"—a chance to enter a trade that might be profitable; and

2. If I was in a trade already, that I might leave the trade too early and miss the maximum profit in the trade, another form of fear of "missing a move".

Seeing many possible qualified trade setups occurring at the same time could lead to a really out of control trading day sometimes for me.

Here are several of the best (worst?) examples of how these trade triggers negatively impacted my trading at times. I rarely trade the GBP/JPY pair—remember the lesson early in my FX trading career when I learned the meaning of "volatility" with this pair? On a day after the world-wide economic meltdown started in 2008, risk aversion was running very high almost every day. Selling risk currencies was in vogue. There was an excellent setup on this pair, based on the principles I was learning from the Coach's Corner classes. The trade had moved almost 200 pips in my favor already, but I knew there was more available.

The trade started early in the morning and the U.S. equity markets were down for the day—nothing unusual at that time. All was looking good on the trade. At lunch, I checked back on the trade and was shocked to see that it was almost back to breakeven. I had not taken partial profits or locked in profits by moving my stop to follow price—it was volatile, after all, and I didn't want to get stopped out before price ran to the deeper profit level I was expecting. So what happened? A Japanese government official, in the middle of the night in Japan, made a statement that Japan's already very low interest rates might need to be lowered even further to stimulate their economy—0% interest rates?? All Yen currency pairs had exploded on this statement and hours of gains were wiped out in minutes. Holding out for those last few pips of gains (didn't want to miss the final move that day) completely backfired. My fear of missing the last move and my desire for a little more profit overrode all logical decisions—such as to lock in profits, scale out on profits or take some steps to make sure the trade saw profit after the huge move it made that day.

The most flagrant example of fear of missing a move came in October, 2008. The United States House of Representatives was set to vote again that day on the legislation that would create the Troubled Asset Relief Program (TARP) to allow the U.S. Government to purchase assets from failing banks. The huge $700 billion stimulus plan was proclaimed to be the salvation of the U.S. economy. The day before the TARP vote was scheduled, I entered a trade on the British Pound, selling Cable and then watching it slide south for hours and hours. The next morning, the day of the vote on TARP, Cable was still sliding in my favor. To that date, this was the biggest size trade I had entered and it was quickly becoming the most profitable trade as well.

I had a price target in mind for the trade which would generate a specific dollar figure in profit which I wanted to achieve for the trade. See the problems already? Sterling's price was continuing to drop still 1 hour before the U.S. equity markets opened for trading. Price continued dropping ever closer to my pre-determined target, so I could achieve the profit that I wanted, not what the market was offering.

Unfortunately, it never made it. Within seconds, tremendous U.S. Dollar selling action began in advance of the assumption that the House of Representatives would pass the TARP bill which the U.S. Senate had already approved. The market's anticipation of the huge U.S. Government spending spree killed the U.S. Dollar for the day and every U.S. major pair rebounded in price and made up for any sell-offs from the prior 24 hours. Almost all of my profits for my "record trade" were gone.

The right-brained emotional trade trigger to hold out and not miss the final move for profits that I set really hurt this time. This trade haunted me and affected my trading for a long time. I replayed the trade over and over again in my mind, just intensifying the negative emotions associated with the trade—the exact opposite of what I should have been doing. Eventually, after using a neuro-linguistic programming technique that Tony Robbins teaches, I was finally able to erase the negative emotions of this great trade that went very, very bad. However, even with the painful emotions of this infamous trade finally resolved, my trade triggers remained hidden in the emotional areas of my brain.

So what should a trader do when the alien trader surfaces through trade triggers? Dr. Steenbarger teaches that the only way to change a vertical split is reprocess the trade triggers. First, discover the trigger.

For me, it was the fear of missing a move for a profit opportunity and the corollary, the fear of not obtaining the maximum profit from an existing trade. I was either trying to be right or trying not to be wrong. Whatever the perspective, either attitude doesn't lead to consistently profitable trading.

I can't count how many times I've had battles in my mind over where to enter a trade if two possible entry levels were available. Opting for the highest entry on a sell or the lowest level on a buy might mean my order doesn't fill and I could miss a profit. Entering at the lowest entry level on a sell or the highest entry level on a buy might mean that I enter too soon, miss some profits and increase my risk in the trade—the dilemmas were endless.

Once the triggers are identified, Dr. Steenbarger discusses in great detail in his DVD presentation three techniques a trader can use to reprocess the trade trigger and the adverse trading behaviors. These behaviors often sabotage trading efforts which then diminishes self-esteem, causing a trader to work even harder to control the undesired behavior—guaranteed to fail.

Unfortunately, the process will continue to repeat itself again and again.

The logic and the simplicity of these three techniques are very compelling; one of these techniques is making a great difference in my trading and how I think about trading. Discovering my trade triggers was 95% of the battle.

I am now very aware of those triggers and I am modifying my trading behavior with the techniques that Dr. Steenbarger teaches. Additionally, I have modified my trading plan to build in safeguards for my trading behaviors which could still surface at times.

The Forex market has daily volume right now of $4 trillion. Obviously, with this size daily market, my trade triggers based on scarcity attitudes make absolutely no sense. With this size market, there is no logical reason to be impatient and not wait for the highest probability trade with the lowest possible risk. As Andrew Jeken, one of the LiveConnect moderators is fond of saying, "the markets will be there tomorrow." Chasing price just to be in a trade is an under-controlled trading behavior and is not high probability trading. Holding out for that last pip as I used to do was not proper trade management. With the exposure based therapy technique that Dr.

Steenbarger teaches, I have been able to reign in my trade triggers and my trading fears of missing the next big move.

Suggested Action Plan:

Review the records of your last 20-30 trades. Are your reasons for entry, exit, trade management and profit taking consistent? Were there any changes in how you how you handled these four issues? What about when the size of the trade increased or when your account value was reaching a new level for you? How about when the profit from a trade hit a new landmark, e.g., the first $500.00, $1000.00, $5000.00, etc. profit in a trade?

If a pattern of unexplained trading behavior surfaces in your trade review, seriously consider resources such as Techniques for Changing Emotional Patterns or Dr. Steenbarger's books and work on identifying the trade triggers that lead to unusual, atypical emotional trading that is holding you back from reaching your trading potential.

Change Your Life In 7 Days - Paul McKenna — The power of controlling your mind to change your outcomes

Kelvin Thornley receives the credit for bringing this book to everyone's attention several months ago in Coach's Corner. This book is laid out to be read in seven consecutive days and focuses on the reader's perception of themselves; It looks at how our brain runs our life. Each day has a homework assignment which is then built on by subsequent days' exercises. This book reads very quickly and contains many examples to explain the important concepts for that day.

There's also a website set up to accompany the book. On the website, there is a thirty minute hypnosis recording. I fell asleep the first few times I listened to it at night, but our brain doesn't stop listening when we take a nap. Right on cue, when the hypnosis was over and it was time to wake up, I did! The exercises in the book are a combination of NLP and hypnosis with an emphasis on the anchoring principle. By going through these exercises daily, I can really feel a difference in my outlook on the day after running through these exercises early in the morning.

I've read this book several times and will keep re-reading it in the future. This book will definitely improve your attitude each day and start the day in the right frame of mind for trading.

Market Wizards - Interviews with Top Traders by Jack D. Schwager — Learning from the best in trading--what was their path to success?

I bought this book after hearing or reading interviews with successful traders who consistently noted that this book turned their trading around. This is very ironic because this trading classic contains interviews with trading legends who were trading failures initially. Some of these traders' trading didn't always look very promising. Although all of these killer traders focus on totally different financial instruments, there are many common themes running through the very detailed interviews that provide extremely valuable lessons.

All of the traders interviewed eventually succeeded because of their persistence. Some of these traders' accounts at one time dwindled to almost nothing—some even blew out their trading accounts and couldn't trade again until they could raise more capital. But rather than giving up, they kept refining their skills and, more importantly, their mental attitudes. They went on to overcome their personal obstacles and rose to the very top of their profession.

These traders frequently cite learning to trade with the trend according to their trading system and not against it (swimming upstream) as the biggest key to their incredible success. From Richard Dennis who turned $400 into $200 million, Marty Schwartz who lost money trading for 10 years, Jim Rogers, Paul Tudor Jones and Ed Sykota, trading with the trend and never giving up ultimately produced incredible trading careers.

The majority of Forexmentor LiveConnect and Coach's Corner trade setups focus on trend trading and not counter-trend trading. Especially for the beginning currency trader, there is no reason to try to swim upstream.

In my early trading, by looking at 5 min, 10 min and 15 min charts, I was constantly fighting the trend present on higher timeframes. I've learned from one successful trader in LiveConnect that he never trades against the 4-hour trend and, if the daily trend is in alignment with the 4-hour trend, then that's even more reason to follow that trend.

Finally, another critical trading attitude that Forexmentor stresses is risk management. It is also one of the keys to the Market Wizards' traders' unbelievable success. Successful trader Larry Hite notes:

> *No matter what information you have, no matter what you are doing, you can be wrong....Never risk more than 1 per cent of total equity on any trade. By risking only 1 per cent, I am indifferent to any individual trade. Keeping your risk small and constant is absolutely critical. (Market Wizards, p.181).*

My earliest exposure to Forexmentor included the repeated discussions about risk management. This was one of the critical keys to becoming consistently profitable. Trade reviews in each session of LiveConnect and Coach's Corner always include discussions of the risk present in each trade and how that risk should be managed. As Larry Hite further explained, "while you can't quantify reward, you can quantify risk." - Market Wizards, p.181. In my coaching session with Vic Noble, risk management was one of the three keys he stressed that I must be consistently applying to my trading.

Reading Market Wizards on a regular basis will keep your trading attitude sharp which is a must to experience long-term and lasting success.

Trading can be an up and down experience, with fighting through the periods where wins don't come easily and losses seem to come too frequently. By becoming emboldened with the knowledge and attitudes of these super successful traders, you will take a big step toward the trading mastery you're seeking.

Suggested Action Plan:

Read Market Wizards several times and take careful notes on the attitudes and thought processes of the traders showcased in this book. In particular, note how they never gave up even in the face of almost total failure. Changes in their approach to trading and in themselves made the difference for them. Regular review of just one interview each week will serve as an excellent check-up on your trading philosophy to catch any negative habits or attitudes that may try to creep into your trading at times. Guard your mind and it will serve you.

The 4 Hour Workweek - Timothy Ferriss — Why living every day more efficiently creates more productive time each day

I learned about this fascinating book from a law school roommate who told me how he was changing his work day and becoming more productive because of what he learned in this book.

The main thrust of the book is to eliminate and simplify. Whether in dealing with meetings, handling email and phone calls, the influence of the media or living daily life, simplify! Tim Ferriss nails these issues head on in this quick read. This is not a book about time management; rather, it's a book about managing your life and the demands that are placed on you. I was already using some of the elimination strategies and techniques from the book, e.g., limiting exposure to media. I've always had the attitude that there was no time to channel surf the TV when that time could be used to learn and to improve myself physically, spiritually and mentally. With Tim's strategies for handling email and phone calls, I am becoming much more productive every day now.

In my trading, the eliminate-and-simplify strategies have brought me back to focusing on trading the British Pound again.

There may be moves in other currencies each day or week, but I'm now maintaining a laser beam focus on Cable and the moves it makes. I've gone from trading valid setups on many currencies where I didn't always have the best feel for support and resistance levels (don't want to miss a move attitude), to slowing down my life and improving the quality of the trades that I'm taking. As a very successful currency said one day in Coach's Corner, there's too much to keep up with if you're only trading one pair exclusively; how can you expect to keep up with the quantity of information needed to successfully trade many pairs? Chasing every pair with a valid set-up can lead to uniformed trading with not too unpredictable results. I've personally had too many Yen pair trades where I had absolutely no comfort level with the trade. I've seen ads for trading platforms from some brokers who boast about the ability to trade over 100 different pairs. Instead of chasing so many "opportunities", find one pair, learn that pair inside and out, improve your trading results and simplify your trading life.

Suggested Action Plan:

The author was earning $40,000 per year with 80 hour work weeks; he now earns $40,000 per month with 4 hour work weeks—buy the book! There are many life strategies in this book that you can use this week to improve the quality of your life and free up time that can be used for other activities such as personal development.

Follow Tim Ferris on Twitter and sign up on his blog. Sign up at: http://www.fourhourworkweek.com/blog/about/ to receive emails only when there's an update—why spend time looking at it daily? Eliminate and simplify!

Forexmentor Resources

A quick review of the tab under Forex Training Resources at www.forexmentor.com quickly reveals the wide extent of currency trading Education information made available to members. As I'm finishing this part of the book in November, 2010, the two newest resources are being released. Frank Paul's Swing Trading course provides training on longer-term trades using Elliott Wave principles and Fibonacci analysis. This system is designed for the trader who doesn't have a lot of time to review charts on a daily basis and is looking for a trading method which does not require a lot of daily attention. The newest program is Shirley Hudson's London Close Trade Strategy. Shirley is a successful realtor and an excellent trader who has developed a trading method with over 90 percent accuracy (winning trades) in the ten months prior to its release. Her trading method, which involves minimal risk, has proven to be predictable and very profitable. In the ten months prior to the release of this program, Shirley accumulated profits of over 3,900 pips – a staggering result. Frank Paul and Shirley Hudson are great examples of the quality of traders who interact with each other every day through Forexmentor (remember the Mastermind principle from Think and Grow Rich?).

Here are the Forexmentor resources which I have found to be the most helpful to my development as a trader:

The Coach's Guide by Vic Noble — 1-on-1 coaching that will immediately improve your daily approach to trading

If I look back and visualize my Forex education journey in a funnel, the 'Big Dogs' course that I started reviewing in April, 2008, would fill in the top of the funnel. There was a vast amount of information that I had to learn initially to succeed in currency trading. First of all, I had to get familiar with how Forexmentor teaches currency trading, the importance of support and resistance on higher timeframes, and the correct way to use technical indicators, pivot points, and buying and selling zones. Once I digested the information from the Toronto seminar with Peter Bain and Steve Nison and completed my review of The Big Dogs course, I needed a system of trading that I could use consistently to apply every day. The Coach's Guide course that Vic Noble recommended to me in late April, 2008, completely met that need.

I still review the set of notes which I made the first time I reviewed The Coach's Guide. These notes are now marked up with post-it notes, yellow highlighter, and notes and comments which I've added over time. (I also started a new set of notes in February, 2010, as if it was my first time to ever see this material – this information is that important). Vic approaches trading in a very consistent method which is easy to learn and to follow.

The concept of market flow, and trend determination as dictated by price completely changed my trading results. Regardless of what financial instrument you trade, as discussed in Market Wizards, trading with the trend is a vital key to success. Again and again, the super traders who are profiled in Market Wizards comment very specifically on this relationship between trading with the trend and their phenomenal success.

In the very first line of my notes that I started taking again on Coachs' Guide on February 17, 2010, my notes start with this question: "What's the path of successful traders?" My notes go on to, again, outline each critical step which successful traders follow as Vic teaches in this course. Later in these notes, I recorded Vic's comments that psychological issues are one of the two biggest stumbling blocks for traders. These issues really should be dealt with before worrying about trading setups. It's this psychological side of life and trading that I've worked on so earnestly with the 7 Day Plan since December, 2009.

If you don't have the Coach's Guide course, this is an absolute must-have for your trading education. Vic teaches traders to focus on approaching trading, managing risk, and the psychological side of trading in a consistent manner. The importance of trading with the trend, selling at resistance and buying at support are universal success concepts in all types of trading, but it is especially so in currency trading. This is material which you will want to, and will need to, review repetitively in order to keep your trading skills sharp.

Coach's Corner — The place to refine your trading skills

Immediately after my private coaching session with Vic, I joined the Coach's Corner (CC). Traders from all over the world meet live on the internet twice a week in a virtual classroom setting to review trades, ask questions, and learn currency trading from Vic. Some sessions feature CC members or special guest speakers. The classes are very interactive with questions and discussions occurring on-the-fly during each class. Every trader walks away from each session closer to the goal of becoming a consistently profitable trader and improving the trading results which they're currently achieving.

Can't attend a CC session on occasion because of work, time-zone issues or because of schedule conflicts? No problem. Every CC session is recorded. There are currently over 400 recordings of past CC sessions. This library of unbelievable trading education is available 24 hours a day to CC members. An index and search engine feature allows quick access to over four years of CC archives so a trader can quickly find answers to trading questions or find a particular trading example. This library of many thousands of hours of detailed training is the "opportunity" that successful people have come into their lives at just the right time.

CC is a place to learn from both winning and losing trades. It is where you can be encouraged to refine your trading skills and to improve the mental skills necessary to succeed at currency trading. With LiveConnect and Coach's Corner, Forexmentor members have unlimited access to the type of mentoring and training that I had no access to when I began my currency trading career.

Weekly Trade Examples by Vic Noble — Learn to trade consistently

Each week, Vic uses a real trading scenario from the past week to illustrate a particular aspect of currency trading. This 5-7 minute video is broadcast to all members each Friday. Topics may include a recent trade setup, risk and trade management, support and resistance, etc. As with the emails from Vic on my own trades where he critiques and makes suggestions about how I could have better handled each trade, these weekly trade example emails are a very important addition to my own learning library. During slow trading days, weekends or holidays, I review these emails and always manage to uncover ideas to help me become more successful. In fact, I've recently started reviewing one weekly trade video each day.

More importantly, as with Vic's interviews with successful traders, I use these weekly trade videos for another purpose. I pay attention to the tone of voice, the posture, the attitude, and the trading philosophies contained in each of the videos. Even if I closed my eyes and didn't watch a single chart, the audio portion of these weekly videos contains information which is very important to building and maintaining the correct mental attitude necessary for consistently profitable trading. There have been many instances in the last few years where, by recalling statements I've heard on these videos during a live trade, I was able to make better trading decisions. Even though these trade videos focus on trades which have already played out, they are an incredible teaching tool for future trades.

Forexmentor LiveConnect by Jarratt Davis — Daily coaching at its best

Every day, the LiveConnect (LC) moderators post the pre-London and pre-New York videos which highlight key support and resistance levels, qualified trade setups, relevant economic news, and other important issues for the upcoming trading session. Just a quick review of these 8 to 10 minute videos gets a trader up to speed on currency market developments for the day. Even if I'm not awake for the start of the

European market (in the middle for the night for me), I can quickly review the pre-London video when I start my day to determine if price reacted to any important support and resistance levels that morning. If so, a trading opportunity may exist by way of a "Noble entry" for example. The pre-New York video is posted around 8:00 a.m. Eastern and updates the London video and provides the latest information to keep traders current before the New York session starts. Periodic review of price charts is videotaped and available for review as another learning opportunity.

Except for a brief period before the start of the New York session, a moderator is always available in the LiveConnect room to answer questions regarding price action, chart patterns, etc. The moderator's post qualified trade setups (not trade recommendations) to keep LC members current.

LiveConnect is an excellent example of the mastermind concept in action. LC presents an exceptional opportunity to learn from experienced, successful traders. LC members can make huge strides toward consistently profitable trading if they will apply the daily reinforcement of the principles taught in LC.

Coach's Corner and Live Connect Members — The Master Mind concept in action--use it to benefit your trading

In Think and Grow Rich, the mastermind concept is defined as "coordination of knowledge and effort, in a spirit of harmony, between two or more people, for the attainment of a definite purpose." Think and Grow Rich, pages 168-169. This is the real value of CC/LC membership. CC and LC members are an incredible asset. Each member has distinct life and trading experiences that they bring to the table to share with other members. CC and LC members live all over the world with diverse professions and backgrounds. Even with different levels of trading experience, members teach, encourage and support each other. On countless occasions, I've seen several people take the exact same trade on a currency pair, but for totally different reasons. This is a fantastic learning opportunity to see different points of view for the next time that particular set-up may occur.

The more points of view that I've seen in chart review and in trade review, the better equipped I am to seeing more set-ups in the future. There is no guarantee of profitability, of course, but being able to locate the set-ups more quickly gives me more opportunities to locate high probability trade set-ups in the future.

CC/LC members learn from and teach each other every day.   Through the LiveConnect room and Coach's Corner sessions, members interact with each other, Vic Noble or the LC moderators on trade set-ups, trades in progress, completed trades, trading philosophies, or any other aspect of currency trading. CC/LC members always work hard to help each other become consistently profitable traders. CC/LC members have taught me many new ways to enter trades, how to manage those trades, how to scale in and out of trades and how to review charts to find high probability trades. I learn something new about trading every time I listen to CC/LC members.

Tactical FX Trend — The key to the success of the super traders in Market Wizards

Think back to Market Wizards. One of the important keys that the super successful traders follow is to trade with, not against, the prevailing market trend. Great concept, but how is the prevailing trend determined? With this course from Vic Noble and Kelvin Thornley, Kelvin introduce a simple method for determining trend by not looking at hard to understand oscillators or technical indicators, but by price action only. Once trend is determined, it becomes just a matter of looking for a trader's edge, the qualified set-up that they trade, and then managing the trade. Vic and Kelvin's course covers both of these issues in detail in the course and in actual trade examples which are posted on the Forexmentor website.

I've seen the principles in this course turn around the trading fortunes of several traders already. I use these principles myself to clarify the prevailing trend as a check on my decision as to which way I'm going to trade Cable on a particular day. The trade management videos, which come with the course, are especially helpful in showing how to remove risk from a trade and how to lock in profits and then close out a trade.

The Support and Resistance course from Vic Noble is a companion course. The principles in the Support and Resistance course are the foundation for many of the trade set-ups which Forexmentor teaches. Two of my sons have told me that they are interested in learning about currency trading. This course will be the first information that they review to learn the basics of trading around key support and resistance levels. This course offers detailed explanations about risk management, how to determine the important support and resistance levels based on chart review, how to conduct a correct top down analysis, how to determine trading confluences using pivots, Fibonacci, and technical indicators and trade issues including entry, stops, and profit-taking levels. Combined with the information in the Tactical Trading course, the Support and Resistance course arms a Forex trader with the information they need to learn in order to identify the trend and to locate the important support and resistance price levels for high probability trading. Using their "edge" as Mark Douglas calls it, the trader can proceed with confidence and move toward trading mastery over time.

Face the Trader Within by Chris Lori — Who are you as a trader?

This is a short, but very important, article that Chris wrote on the psychological battles that all traders must conquer. Every trader has a unique background because of their life experiences, educational background, occupation, and trading successes/failures so far. Chris focuses on risk management (as with all Forexmentor programs and as mentioned by the superstar traders in Market Wizards), the importance of discipline in trading, determining who you are as a trader, and filtering the volumes of "expert opinions" about the markets and being responsible for your own trading decisions.

Chris' background as an Olympic athlete really comes through with the thoroughness and the details in each area of the article—this is something to read several times and then re-read again. Face The Trader covers many of the important psychological and success habits that successful traders follow—having a specific trading plan, following that plan, recognizing the probabilities present in the currency markets and knowing themselves as a trader and where they fit in the market—does their trading plan fit with their personality?

This article is packed with information crucial to developing strength as a trader on the mental side of trading.

The Secret and the Missing Secret — Use the Law of Attraction right now to reach your goals

After hearing about the movie "The Secret" from several successful people (remember, success leaves clues), I began searching for the movie at our local movie stores. It took a few tries, but it was worth the effort. As with all other personal development materials, The Secret is not something to watch only one time and then put it away. Similar to the funnel analogy I used in discussing my history of Forex trading education, the first time I watched this movie, I understood the general concepts. Every subsequent viewing of the movie narrows the focus and refines the thoughts in the movie into clear, extremely valuable principles which can be applied to goal setting and goal achievement in all areas of life.

The Secret features over fifty "teachers", personal development names such as Bob Proctor, Jack Canfield, John Assaraf, Dennis Waitley and Joe Vitale. They discuss the critical elements of how to set and achieve goals using the Law of Attraction. The Law of Attraction is "the mighty law that draws to us the things we desire or fear, that makes or mars our lives." Thought Vibration, William Walker Atkinson, p. 3.

According to the Law of Attraction, the subconscious carries out the orders and instructions that are given to it by the conscious mind, i.e., the subconscious is the software that runs our lives. Atkinson describes this power this way: "Strong expectancy is a powerful magnet. He of the strong, confident desire attracts to him the things best calculated to aid him—persons, things, circumstances, surroundings; if he desires them hopefully, trustfully, confidently and calmly." Thought Vibration, p.39. In Think and Grow Rich, Napolean Hill summarizes this process as Ask, Believe (with emotion) and Receive.

Here's the best explanation of this principle:

> *Then Jesus told them, "I tell you the truth, if you have faith and don't doubt, you can do things like this and much more. You can even say to this mountain, 'May you be lifted up and thrown into the sea,' and it will happen. You can pray for anything, and if you have faith, you will receive it" Matthew 21:21-22.*

The Secret goes through each step necessary in the process of formulating and achieving goals in health, finances, relationships and all other areas of life. The Secret explains how the great inventors, business leaders, and other people have used these steps to change history throughout the ages. The movie itself was completed using these principles.

When Rhonda Byrne was at a point where she was struggling in her personal life, a friend of Rhonda's gave her a copy of the 1910 book The Science of Getting Rich by Wallace D. Wattles. (Bob Proctor discusses this book extensively in his Science of Getting Rich Program). Based on what she learned in this book, Rhonda began researching principles and rules of success, similar to Napolean Hill's quest that lead to the book Think and Grow Rich. With a minimal budget and no definite filming schedule, she came to the United States with only one interview arranged for the movie.

Rhonda and her film crew focused on and attracted the right people that they need to complete the movie. The manner in which the movie came together, finished and was ultimately marketed to the world exemplify how successfully the principles of ask, believe and receive can be applied.

One of the teachers or speakers featured in the movie was Joe Vitale.

Joe is considered to be one of the top marketing experts in the world. He is a highly-respected speaker and has authored very many bestselling books and audio programs (www.mrfire.com). According to Joe, as discussed in his audio program "The Missing Secret," what we have in our lives right now is the result of what we have attracted into it. The subconscious programs and beliefs that we hold are manifesting themselves in the life that we are experiencing right now. In order to change what we are currently experiencing, these programs and beliefs will have to be "cleared" or removed in order for the law of attraction to allow new realities to take place.

Through repeated listening (several times per week for many weeks) and by working through the exercises in The Missing Secret, this program helped me find out why I have certain trading behaviors. I knew from Brett Steenbarger's DVD seminar (which I've referenced to earlier) that I had a tendency to trade impulsively for fear of "missing a move", a chance to enter a trade that could be profitable or that I might exit a trade too early and not realize maximum profit. Because of The Missing

Secret, I've learned that I have subconscious programs and beliefs from prior experiences in my life that were negatively impacting my trading analysis and trade management decisions at times. These programs/beliefs would especially rear their ugly heads as I approached specific trading account values ("I'm almost to X dollars"), as I was on a winning streak with my trades ("I'm due for a loss"), or as momentum was building in an existing trade ("it's early, there's probably a lot more potential than the profit target I set before the trade began.").

Because of these subconscious programs/beliefs, I can now understand why I've acted outside of my usual trading patterns (the Steenbarger vertical split discussed previously) in deciding to impatiently enter trades or manage trades once entry occurred. Early in my trading, many of these mistakes were attributable to not having a consistent setup that I was trading and from not understanding the importance of trend and higher timeframe support and resistance. If these mistakes were to occur now, lack of experience is not the explanation. Rather, my subconscious programs are sabotaging my trading and standing in the way of achieving my full potential as a trader. By removing or "clearing" these programs as Joe refers to them, I can break through these barriers and change the results that I'm achieving right now and reach the possibilities available in my trading.

Tony Robbins talks about the thermostat-like nature of our subconscious. This is the way our minds can cool things off if we get too hot (e.g., a new high account value, being in the most profitable trade ever, being in a bigger trade than we're used to trading, etc.). Only by clearing any limiting subconscious programs, as Joe teaches, can an athlete, actor, author, student, businessman/woman or trader reach a new level of accomplishment.

Joe's Missing Secret program very logically walks the listener through the understanding necessary to first pinpoint the subconscious limitations and, more importantly, how to address these programs (thermostats) so they can be resolved once and for all and the listener can begin to be, have and accomplish all they desire.

Once limiting beliefs are dissolved, actions are then guided by Divine inspiration and not by programs instilled in the subconscious by the media, family, teachers, friends, etc. This book is an example of that type of inspiration. I am not an author and never particularly excelled at English classes in school. In the process of reviewing Joe's Missing Secret program and in working through clearing exercises he teaches, I received the Divine inspiration to write this book. The first draft of the entire book was completed in less than 2 months. As Joe teaches, actions taken after inspiration are effortless—that has been very true with this book.

By writing this book, I've learned and relearned many countless valuable lessons about how I approached my trading in the past and how I will approach trading in the future to reach even greater levels of success.

I've really learned how I approach trading mentally, what has worked and not worked for me and what I must do to continue to improve this very important side of my trading in the future. Because it was driven by inspiration, writing this book has not been hard. Writing this book at this time, over 1 year after starting the 7 Day Plan, has given me a renewed focus on reaching the many goals I've established for the next 1, 3, 5 and 10 years.

Ashraf Laidi – Applying intermarket analysis to excel in Forex trading

Intermarket Analysis is the study of the relationships that financial markets have between and on each other. When trading currencies, it's critical to consider the role of currencies, commodities, and equity markets on each other. Another benefit I received from attending the Toronto seminar in April, 2008, was my introduction to the intermarket analysis which Ashraf Laidi provided for CMC Markets clients. A CMC representative was at the Toronto seminar to provide information about their brokerage services. At that time, CMC conducted business in the United States, so I opened an account with them just to have access to Ashraf's analysis each day. I've mentioned earlier in this book all of the resources, websites, and market information I was pouring over every day when I began trading currencies to try get up to speed on the worldwide financial markets. Even if I was able to assemble or collect all of the data on the various financial markets and price movement, along with economic news developments, I still had to determine how all of this information related to each other and how it might affect my trading. After following Ashraf Laidi for almost 3 years now, and learning from his extremely perceptive analysis of the financial markets, I'm learning the critical importance of the relationships of all of the various markets to each other and how price movement or a development in one market will impact other markets.

Unfortunately, not long after the Toronto seminar, CMC closed its U.S. operations. I was no longer a CMC client with access to Ashraf's daily analysis updates. However, the learning and information flow did not stop just because CMC closed its U.S. offices. Ashraf has now developed a website at www.ashraflaidi.com. On April 1, 2011, Ashraf resigned from CMC Markets to focus on his website and operate as an

Independent Global Markets Strategist. His website's subtitle – "Incisive Global Markets Analysis" is an understatement, to say the least. After only one visit to his website, I'm convinced that you'll never go a day without this information as you trade currencies. Ashraf provides many ways to follow his extremely accurate analysis of economic and geo-political news and currency trends around the world. He provides periodic e-mails (Intraday Market Thoughts) throughout the day. These e-mails continue late into the night, in the early morning hours, and even into the weekend if news developments merit. He conducts live seminars around the world as well as webinars on the internet. The last webinar presentation I attended was a five-plus hour discussion of currency trends and psychological trading issues with Ashraf and Chris Lori. The weekend webinar cost less than $50.00 to attend, and this small investment of money and several hours of my time paid off very quickly in my trading results because of Ashraf's analysis on currencies and Chris' very thorough discussion of trading psychology issues.

The development of Twitter has made e-mail as a method of communicating very slow. In the last year, Ashraf has provided over 7,000 tweets at all hours of the day, during holidays, and on weekends. I have seen many tweets from Ashraf mere seconds after a news release setting out his correct analysis of the news item and how it will directly impact the markets and currencies that day, the rest of the week or for weeks and months in the future. Ashraf is not providing a trade alert service with entries and exits recommendations. However, his ability to identify important support and resistance levels, critical trend lines, fibonacci resistance or support levels, and potential price targets for a currency is incredibly uncanny. With tweets, Ashraf often refines price level analysis throughout the trading day or week if conditions change. He provides short-term, medium-term, and long-term analysis of equities, currencies, and commodities. For example, he analyzes gold, silver, oil, the S&P 500, the Dow, other equity markets around the world and numerous currency pairs. Ashraf uses analysis combinations which I've never seen discussed by any other analyst. At the time that I'm writing this book, Ashraf has recently correctly called a short-term top in many Euro currency pairs; and among those pairs, he pointed out the higher probability pairs to trade. He also recently discussed a head-and-shoulders pattern on the S & P/VIX ratio, a ratio which I've never seen reviewed by any media analyst. The frequency of Ashraf's tweets, and the fact that they come at all times of the day and night, confirm Ashraf's commitment and dedication to his profession and to the advanced education which he provides at no cost to those who are looking for the absolute best and most up-to-date information in foreign exchange trading.

Ashraf does not linger in the "fluff" that's common for television financial analysts. His understanding of the interplay between equities, currencies, and commodities and where this interplay will cause prices to go make review of his analysis extremely important for Forex traders.

Ashraf's 2008 book "Currency Trading and Intermarket Analysis" is required reading for any currency trader. His book has been ranked Number 1 in Amazon's Foreign Exchange and Finance subcategories. This New York Times Best Seller is kept current through his website with an online workbook (very small subscription fee) and the frequent online articles posted on his website (over 100 already). Ashraf also keeps his analysis current through "Hot Charts" (technical analysis and discussion of currently trending currencies).

In summary, I've not found a better way to stay on top of quick-moving developments in the currency markets. A trader still must review the information which Ashraf provides and consider where that information fits in their trading plan and then make their own trading decisions accordingly.

However, for the best in detailed, extremely accurate intermarket analysis information which is necessary to begin the process of making a decision whether to enter a trade, Ashraf Laidi is an amazing and reliable resource. There's a clear reason why he already has over 12,000 Twitter followers.

Suggested Action Plan:

First, purchase Ashraf's book and study this book to learn how worldwide financial markets are so intertwined now. Review Ashraf's book daily to absorb the thought process involved with intermarket analysis. Second, subscribe to Ashraf's IMTs on his website and review each IMT to reinforce the concepts which Ashraf teaches. Third, sign up to follow Ashraf on Twitter and review his tweets each day to stay current on economic and international news developments which can impact your currency trading. Finally, continuously review Ashraf's website and take advantage of the many resources he offers on the site to increase your knowledge of the Forex markets.

VII. Change Your Perspective

How to Start Your 7 Day Plan — Why and How to work diligently on yourself to take your life and trading to a new level

The purpose of personal development is to constantly expose yourself to new ideas, attitudes, beliefs or philosophies to positively improve your personal, professional or financial life. Pull up the website for Federal Express (www.fedex.com). In a recent webinar I attended, the speaker asked everyone to take a close look at this logo and I'll ask you to do the same. What do you notice about the logo? Just a group of letters making up the company name; correct? Now look a little closer…is there an image there which symbolizes what this company does every day? Look between the "E" and the "x" (the arrow pointing to the right—signifying action). Since I became aware of the arrow, when I see a FedEx truck on the road, I now see this symbol before I see the collection of letters—my perspective has changed because of new information—this is the goal of engaging in personal development in your life.

Jim Rohn defines success as "practicing a few simple disciplines every day". He goes on to say that discipline is the "bridge between thought and accomplishment." Paul Martinelli offers daily motivational emails at his website www.paulmartinelli.net. His Daily Thought the day I wrote this chapter was: "Anyone who has never made a mistake has never tried anything new." The process of learning currency trading, like any other new skill or profession, can be riddled with mistakes at first—it happens. If those mistakes become learning lessons though, then mistakes can become the stepping stones toward increased knowledge to use in the future. Adding the discipline of personal development can be the final missing piece of the puzzle in your trading.

Here's a sample of a typical day for my personal development activities. I'm listing these activities to give you an idea of how to fill your day with activities which will, over time, make a tremendous difference in your life and in your trading:

Early morning: Mind Movies	5 mins
Review Martinelli/Nightingale Conant	3-4 mins
Daily thoughts/John Maxwell Minutes	
Review short, medium and long-term goals	3-5 mins
Visualization/NLP practice (7 Days book)	10-20 mins
Write out/visualize key trading rules	2 mins
Chart review, review of overnight news/news analysis	15-30 mins
Driving time (day)—tapes/CDs (might be 3-6 hours some days)	60-70 mins
Lunch: Review goals and key trading rules; reading	5-20 mins
Evening: Exercise	30 mins
Review short, med., long-term goals	4 mins
Mind Movies	5 mins
Review trade examples	5 mins

| Reading | 15-30 mins |
| Add to gratitude list | 1-2 mins |

Throughout the day, I may also review index cards with one or two goals or key thoughts on them. As I mentioned in the discussion of Mind Movies, I have an anchor that I use to fire certain images about my goals. I also have other anchors that I've set up with NLP exercises. These anchors may take only seconds at a time and they happen at various times during the day.

The early morning and late evening are when the subconscious is the most receptive to suggestions, goals and visualization because of the presence of theta brain waves. This is why these activities are clustered in those times of the day.

Weekends are used for more reading and taking notes; review of videos on weekly trade examples from Vic, from LiveConnect or review of trader interviews; workouts (also during the week); visualization practice, goal review and chart review to prepare for the following week.

To get started on your own 7 Day Plan, you first need an accountability partner—someone to whom you will provide your weekly plan each week. A friend who trades, a spouse who supports your trading activities or someone who is successful in their career who practices discipline in their daily life already are excellent accountability partners. Also, consider using Bob Proctor's master mind groups and www.bobproctormastermindgroups.com as another resource for a partner.

Next, where are you heading in your life and in your trading? Do you have a set of written goals? Statistics reveal that only 3% of people have written goals—be among the few that have a written plan for what they will accomplish. Jim Rohn's goal setting exercise in The Art of Exceptional Living is excellent; Zig Ziglar also has an entire audio program on setting and achieving goals. It may take 10-20 hours to work through and refine your short, medium and long-term goals. However, I've found that I have time to accomplish my busy daily agenda because I've taken the time to set my goals. By having a set of well-defined, specific goals I'm much more motivated every day. Also, I have the energy I need to achieve the daily goals that will help me reach the big goals. By setting goals and focusing on why I want to accomplish each goal, my goals actually drive my actions every day now. Setting goals will unquestionably give you more time in your day.

With goals on paper, now what do you need to work on to get there?

For me, the first changes I made were to sleep and exercise more and trade less—I ended up with much improved trading results. I felt better physically and was able to make better decisions mentally throughout the day with this combination of changes. Determine specifically what aspect of trading you want to work on each week— entries, exit, better management, etc?

You need time for exercise each week and you can always listen to audio courses while exercising, a great way to double-up on personal development time. Find books to read and CDs to review (recommendations are in the Bibliography), review the trading resources that Forexmentor offers each week with actual trade videos, trade tutorials, the trader interviews, and the many courses. Review these materials often; constant review of quality materials is the path to the 10,000 hours required to develop trading mastery.

Decide how you will practice visualization (Mind Movies creates the "theatre in your mind" that Maxwell Maltz advocates). How will you review your goals each day? Possibilities include index cards around your house and in your car or a journal that you carry with you all the time so you can review it during free times in the day/at lunch/breaks from work.

There are endless resources available on the internet; many are free. Webinars on personal development and psychological trading issues occur every week. (I just received an email today about a Chris Lori webinar on the 7 Characteristics of a Forex Professional). Be realistic with your plan and find the right balance between being too easy on yourself and over-committing to too many activities each week—this has been my biggest challenge. My busy family life can make it very difficult for me to reach my goals some weeks, but having to push myself every day has forced me to grow in many areas of my life.

Finally, if you have any questions on any of the information in this book or would like help putting together your 7 Day/personal development plan, please feel free to contact me at irishgolf.deming@gmail.com.

In Zig Ziglar's program on setting goals, he makes a comment that he believes that everyone should write a book---I absolutely agree! Writing this book has forced me to really examine how I think as a trader, my beliefs about trading and what I can work on to become more consistent in my trading. After gathering all of the 7 Day materials that I've reviewed so intensively for over one year, going back over my currency trading career and where Forexmentor has brought me in almost 3 years, and then writing down my thoughts in this book, I'm ready for 2011. The goals that I've set for myself this year are very ambitious. Just a few months into the year, I've made big strides toward reaching these goals already. I'm building momentum for the rest of this year. I'm looking forward to making even more positive changes in my life, becoming more organized and being even more committed to continuing on the road toward 10,000 hours and beyond. How many hours have I logged so far? I have no idea. Am I close to that magic 10,000 hour level? Not yet. Will I be a lot closer when it's time to review 2011 and set new goals for 2012? Definitely! With the 7 Day Plan, every day brings me closer to where I want to be with my life and my trading. If I can help you in any way, it would be my great pleasure to do so.

Drive safe and trade well!

Dave Deming

Charts and Figures

Figure 1

Figure 2

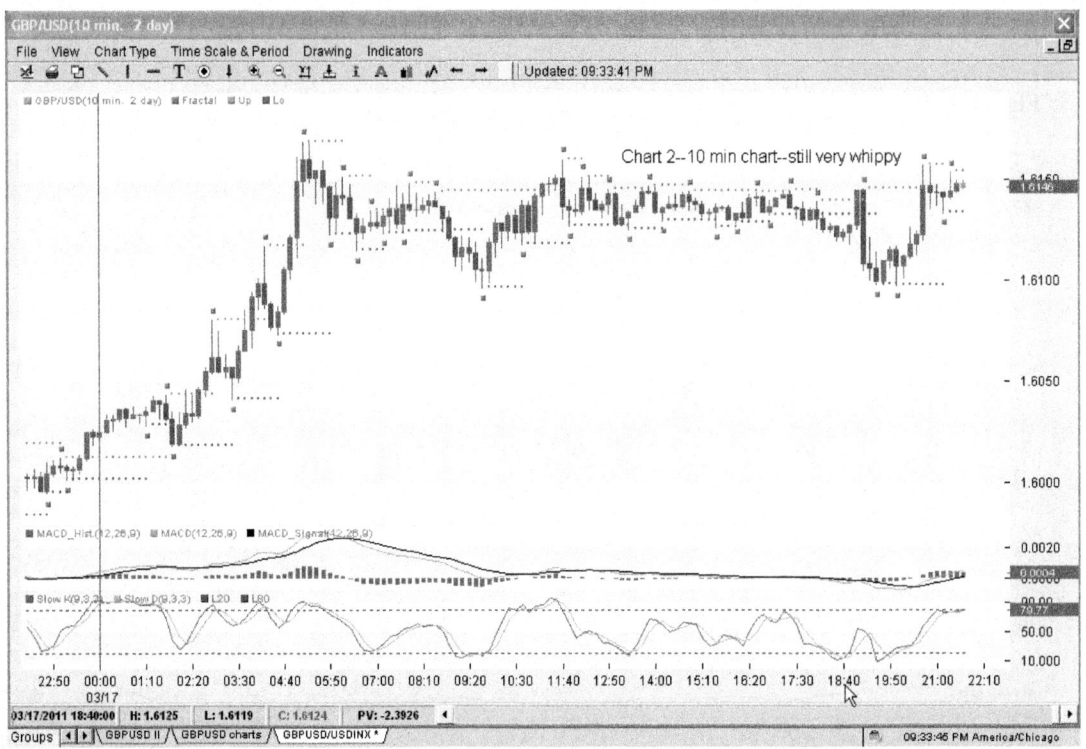

Figure 3

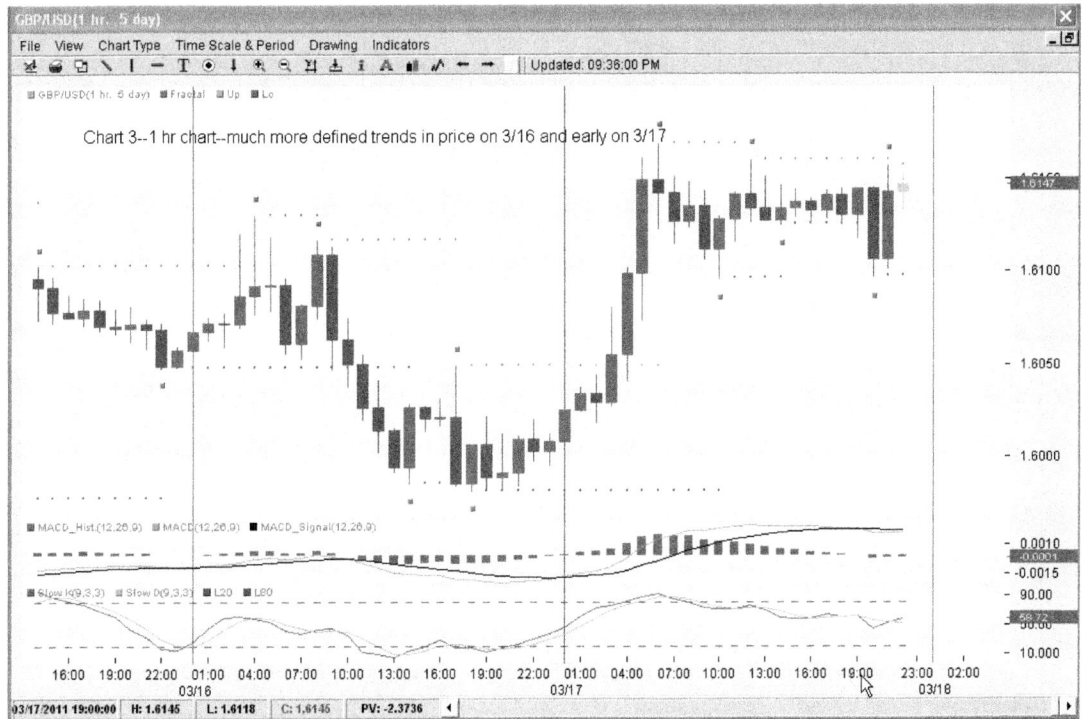

Figure 4

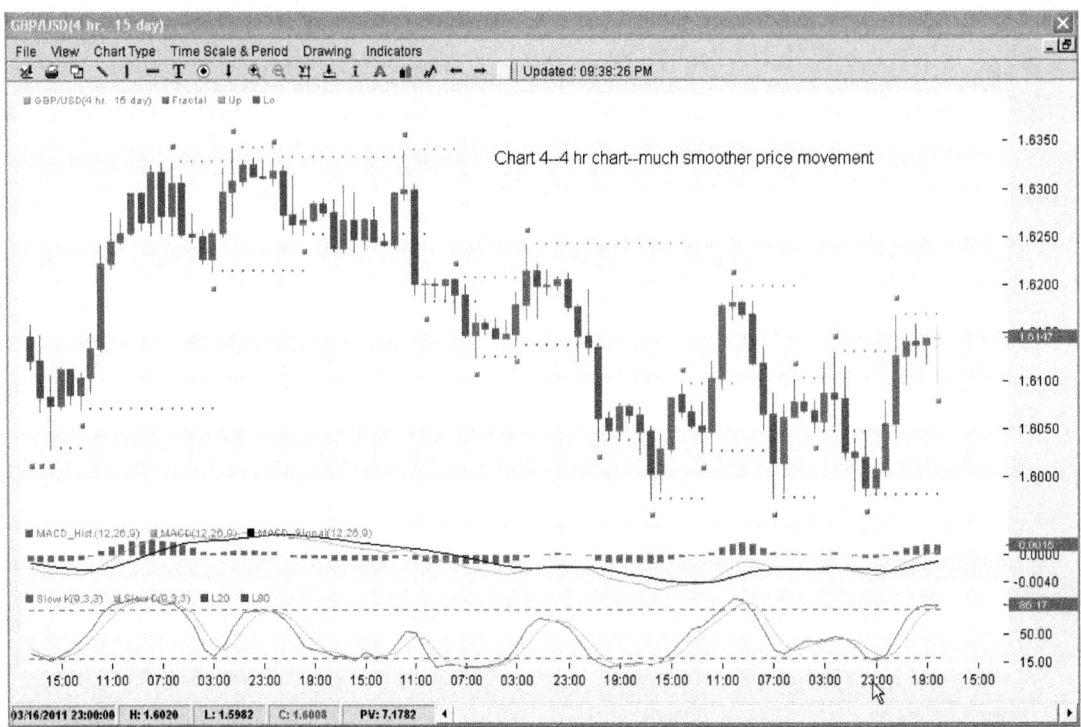

Driving Your Way to Success

Figure 5

Figure 6

Date ___8/14-7___
Pair ___GBP/CHF___

Trending:
S/R
Rising/Falling S/R lines (less important)
ADX >25
RSI, MACD, Stoch all in the same direction? **Any divergence?
Fib. Lines
MA-10/20/50/100/200
Risk reversals table
7 day rule?

Range:
ADX <20
RSI/Stoch (any divergence?)
B. Bands-low volatility?
S/R   S 2.4225   R 2.4337
MACD
Risk Reversals table

(handwritten, right side)
Daily ↑   RSI 41   ADX 26.2
4h ↑
Hourly RSI 63.38   32.8

Risk/Reward: T₁ 2.433 (+71)/(+113)??? 1) high wave — H at 8/0
  Candle review—Target 2.4377 Why? m, of Bull discourage day
  S/L level ___2.4234___   2 day low/Parabolic SAR/Other   7!
  Time loss for trade? _____
  Reserve needed for stop move ___30___
  2% account loss figure _____
  Any reversal signals near current price? _____
  _____

  Is trade anticipating/reacting? _____
    Why not? Why are probabilities good for trade? _____
    _____

  Any impending news? _____

Time Frame for Trade: Intraday (Hourly, RSI/Stoch, BB, Fib levels)
              Medium-term (Daily, indicators as above + Fib levels)

Entry: ___2.4264___
Exit: _____
Profit/Loss: _____

Comments:

Figure 7

	10:04	8/15 5:06	5:30	6:03	8:00	9:38 +41	11:42 -3	12:37	3:05	d:01
USD/JPY	117.38/41	116.69/72	72/75	66/69	74/78	117.31/34	26/29	41/45	116.73/76	59/63
GBP/USD	1.9926/30	1.9895/98	94/98	97/00	71/75	1.9925/29	27/30	38/41	13/17	87/93
GBP/JPY	233.92/99	232.15/22	23/30	16/22	232.00/10	233.67	66/73	234.09/18	232.44/54	231.84/98
EUR/USD	1.3522/26	3490/93	86/89	77/79	62/65	82/85	71/74	72/75	51/54	40/43
AUD/USD	8315/18	8240/43	32/35	41/44	09/13	48/50	40/43	41/44	15/18	48/02
NZD	7208/12	7155/59	47/51	51/56	34/39	75/79	57/61	79/83	23/28	7099/03
GBP/CHF	2.4142/50	2.4132/36	54/57	63/68	85/90	68/70	84/91	08/14	2.4262/69	61/51
EUR/AUD	1.6259/67	1.6369/77	74/82	48/56	53/01	1.6344/53	43/51	43/52	69/76	6392/01
AUD CHF	1.0094/78	.9993/98	95/99	08/12	92/17	1.0040/47	41/45	48/53	1.0009/14	99.93/99
AUD JPY	97.60/65	96.15/20	13/18	17/22	95.86/90	96.71/76	63/68	75/80	95.85/90	95.57/63
USD/CHF	1.2113/17	1.2127/30	41/44	43/46	71/74	76/79	84/88	91/95	82/86	92/96

Figure 8

			GBP$--Close for week
■	Jan 10 2008	5.25%	1.9541
■	April 10, 2008	5.0%	1.9946
■	Oct 8, 2008	4.5%	1.7302
■	Nov 6, 2008	3.0%	1.4797
■	Dec 4, 2008	2.0%	1.4945
■	Jan 8, 2009	1.5%	1.4744
■	Feb 5, 2009	1.0%	1.4400
■	March 5, 2009	0.5% and 75B QE	1.3975
■		("increase money supply and credit")	
■	5/7/2009	0.5% and QE to $125B	1.5164
■	8/6/2009	0.5% and QE to $175B	1.6528
■	11/5/2009	0.5% and QE to $200B	1.6692
■			Close for the
■	11/4/2010	0.5% and QE to $200B	week is 1.6135

Figure 9

Figure 10

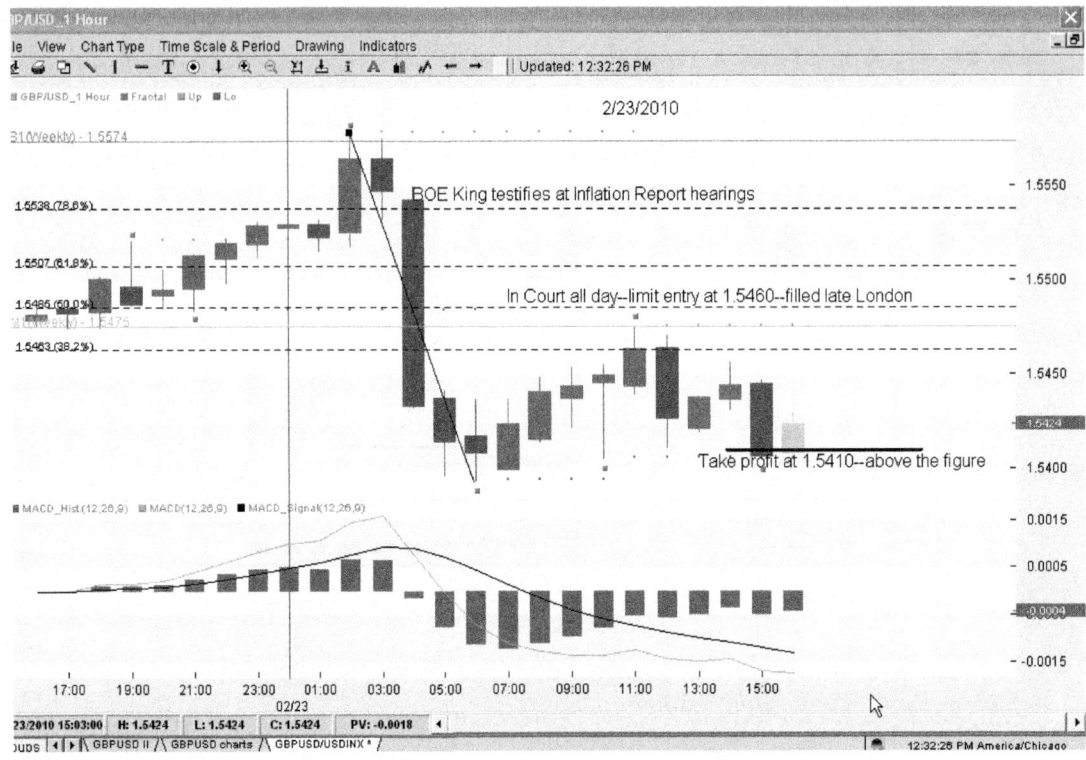

Figure 11

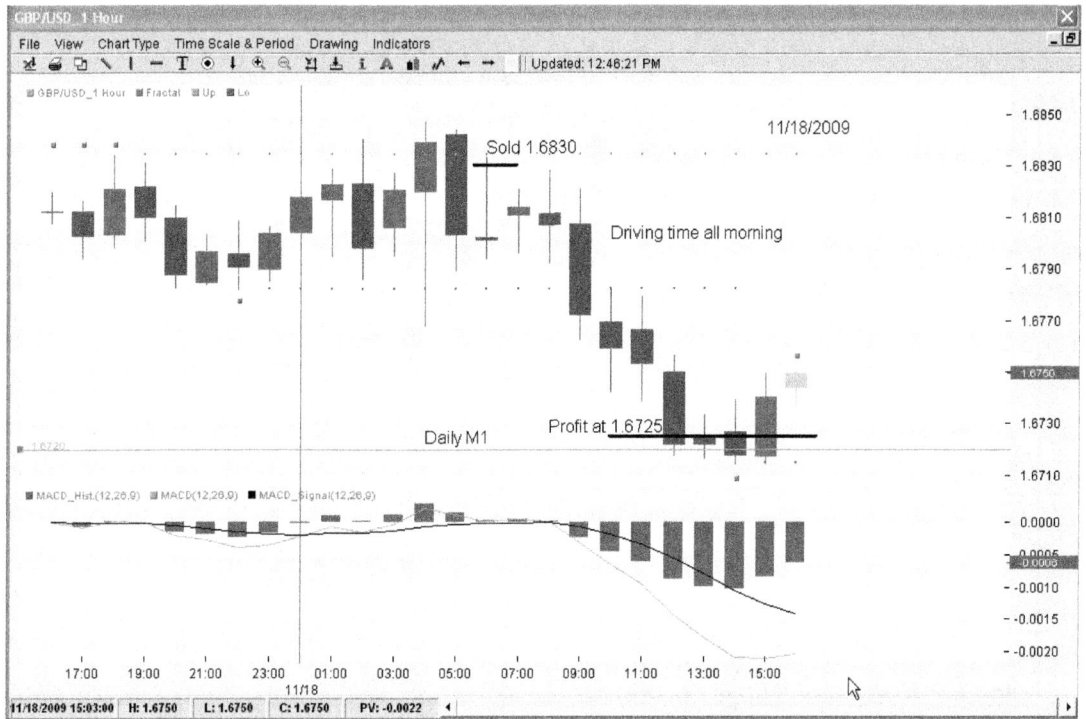

Figure 12

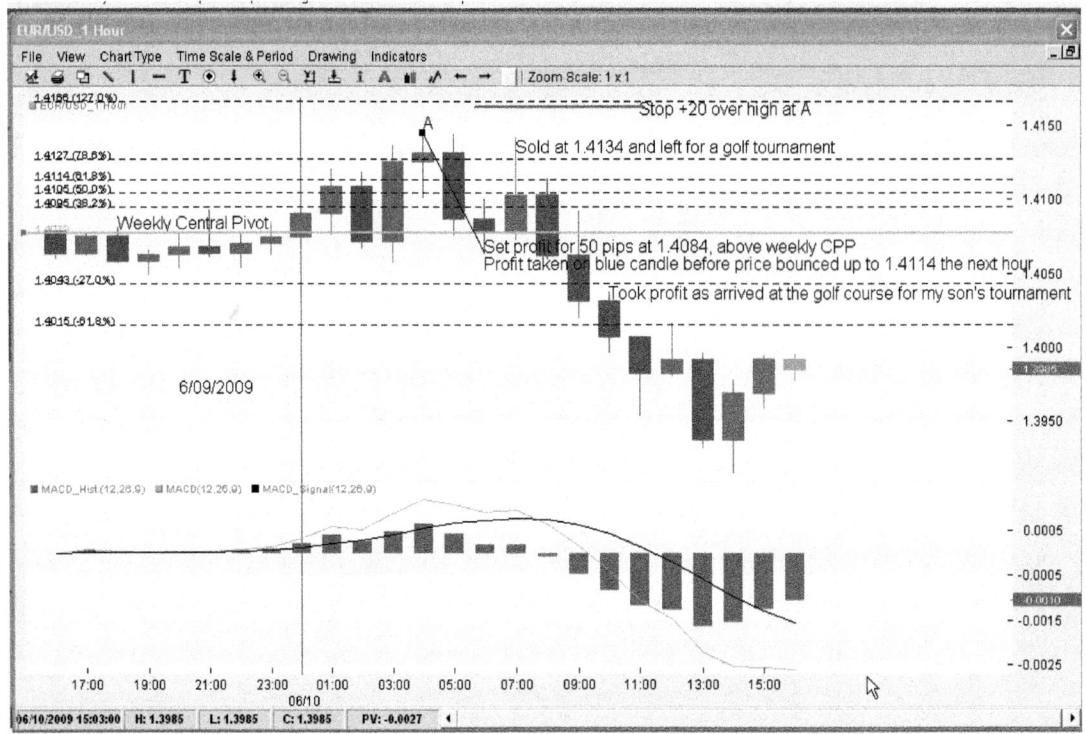

Figure 13

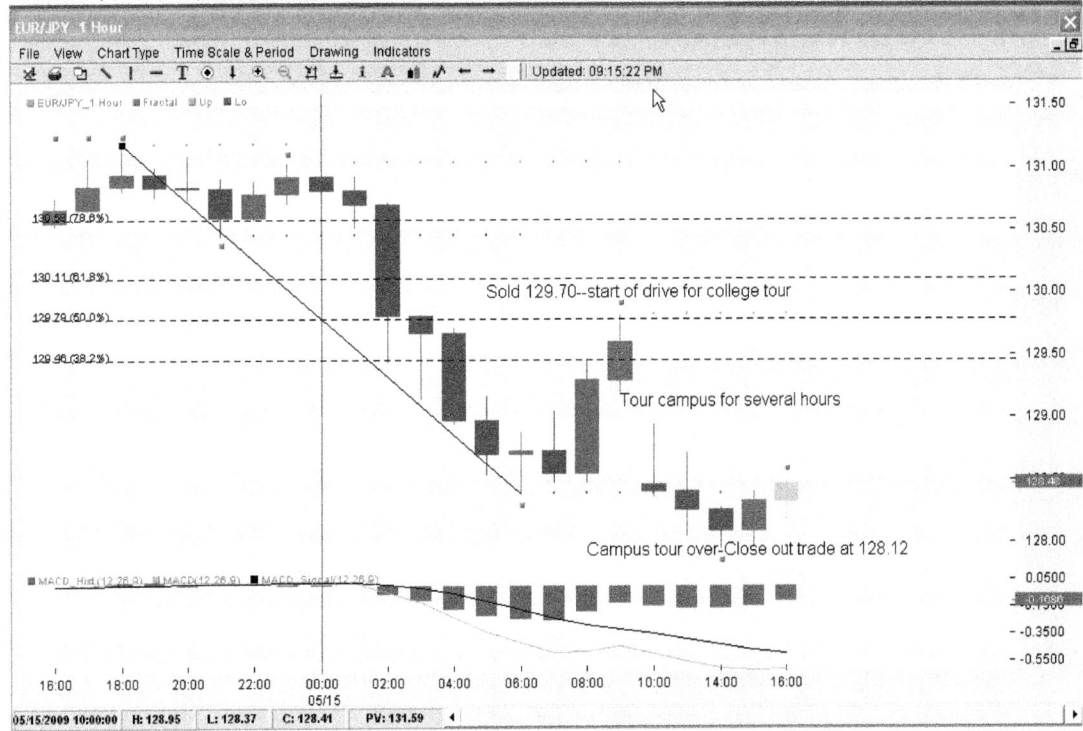

Bibliography of Recommended Personal Development Resources

The resources marked with *** are highly recommended. These are resources that should be key parts of your learning library.

(This resource list will be updated with new recommendations at: http://drivingdave.blogspot.com)

*** Allen, James: As a Man Thinketh (1904)

Canfield, Jack and Hansen, Mark Victor - The Aladdin Factor Berkley Books (1995)

Chu, Chin-Ning: Do Less, Achieve More - Harper Collins (1998)

Clason, George S.: The Richest Man in Babylon - Penguin Books (1955)

Davies, Bob: The Sky Is Not the Limit, You Are! - In-Fact Publishing Co. (1994)

*** Douglas, Mark: Trading In the Zone - Prentice Hall Press (2000)

Ferris, Timothy: The 4-Hour Workweek - Random House, Inc. (2007)

Gawain, Shakti: Creative Visualization - Bantam Books (1978)

Gladwell, Malcom: Outliers - Little Brown & Co. (2008)

Hill, Napolean and Stone, W. Clement: Success Through a Positive Mental Attitude - Simon and Schuster, Inc, (1977)

*** Hill, Napolean: Think and Grow Rich - Ballantine Books (1960)

*** Maltz M.D, Maxwell: The New Psycho-Cybernetics - Prentice Hall Press (2001)

*** McKenna, Paul: Change Your Life in 7 Days - Harmony Books (2004)

Murphy, Dr. Joseph, Ph.D.: The Power of Your Subconscious Mind - Bantam Books (1963)

Newman, James W.: Release Your Brakes! - The J.W.Newman Corporation (1995)

Nison, Steve: The Candlestick Course - John Wiley & Sons, Inc. (2003)

Profiting In Forex - Using Candlesticks to Catch The Next Move DVD course - Candle Charting Essentials and Beyond Vols. 1-4 (http://www.1shoppingcart.com/app/?af=1277658)

NLP - The New Technology of Achievement (audioprogram) (www.nightingale.com)

*** Peale, Norman Vincent: The Power of Positive Thinking - Ballantine Books (1956)

Proctor, Bob: The 11 Forgotten Laws (audio program) (www.the11forgottenlaws.com/?p=3890), The Science of Getting Rich (audio program) (www.irishgolf.thesgr.hop.clickbank.net)

Robbins, Anthony: Awaken the Giant Within - Simon & Schuster (1991), Personal Power II - The Driving Force (audio program), Unlimited Power - Ballantine Books (1986)

*** Rohn, Jim: The Art of Exceptional Living (audio program) (www.nightingale.directtrack.com/z/10646/CD3439)

Schwartz, David J.: The Magic of Thinking Big Prentice-Hall, Inc. (1987)

Smith, Hyrum: The 10 Natural Laws of Successful Time and Life Management Warner Books, Inc, (1994)

Steenbarger, Dr. Brett: A Trader's Guide to Self Discipline: Proven Techniques to Improve Trading Profits (DVD) (www.traderslibrary.com)

The Daily Trading Coach - John Wiley & Sons, Inc. (2009)

Enhancing Trader Performance: Proven Strategies from the Cutting Edge of Trading Psychology - John Wiley & Sons, Inc. (2006)

The Psychology of Trading - John Wiley & Sons, Inc, (2002)

Tharp, Van Disciplined Trading: How to Trade Your Way to Financial Freedom (CD or DVD) (www.traderslibrary.com)

Tracy, Brian: The New Psychology of Achievement (audio program) (www.nightingale.com).

*** Vitale, Joe: The Missing Secret (audio program) Includes Thought Vibration by William Walker Atkinson (www.nightingale.directtrack.com/z/10704/CD3439)

Waitley, Dennis: Psychology of Winning (audio program) (www.nightingale.com)

Ziglar, Zig: Goals, How to Set Them, How to Reach Them (audio program) (www.nightingale.com)

Please note: The fines from the 7 Day Plan are contributed to various charities. Purchases through an affiliate program on any of these resources will be used to help support St. Jude Children's Hospital (www.stjude.org).

CPSIA information can be obtained
at www.ICGtesting.com
Printed in the USA
BVOW07s2140060617

486195BV00004B/186/P